Learn to Run:

A Common Sense Beginner's Guide to Running Progression

Richard Holt & Chris Hall

ISBN: **978-1499699241**

Cover image source photograph kindly provided by Juandevojnikov.

Contents

7. Warming Up, Cooling Down and Stretching

Introduction

For over a decade, Momentum Sports has endeavoured to help people of all shapes, sizes and abilities to take up running, whether as a hobby or as a serious pursuit. In that time we have helped over a thousand athletes from the ages of eight up to seventy-five and from the shortest of sprints to ultra-distance (100 kilometres and more).

Our philosophy during this period has been to build a solid platform for all athletes' running, whether they be total beginners or elite athletes, so that they can develop their performances over time and enjoy their running in the long-term.

This involves building a good base of fitness, some appropriate strength work, a look at technique and lastly planning so that each individual is training at the right level for them.

In this book we aim to help you start to build your enjoyment of running, with a book aimed at the total beginner. It takes you through many of the thought processes and challenges that a novice runner will face and will help you avoid some of the many mistakes that are often made by beginners when they take up this great activity and sport of ours.

We hope you enjoy the book and find that it helps you with your running. At Momentum Sports our senior coaches have an average experience of about 25 years in the sport and are well placed to help you get started. Please feel free to give us any feedback you have on the book at coaches@momentumsports.co.uk

Here's to all the best for your running.

Why Start Running?

Running is one of the most popular hobbies for people of all ages in the United Kingdom, so there must be a few things that pull people towards it! This chapter will briefly discuss the social and personal benefits that taking up running can bring with it, but it will also explore the health and physiological benefits. We all know that taking up running will make us fitter, but do we know exactly what happens to our bodies as we exercise frequently?

Chapter 1

i What are the Benefits of Running?

There are many reasons why people decide to take up running as a hobby. We have listed just a few of them below:

Arguably most importantly, the health benefits of running are massive. As well as the more obvious aspects such as strengthening the heart and enabling a more efficient flow of blood and oxygen around the body, running can be a great cure for stress or even depression.
Part ii of this chapter explores this in more detail.

A lot of people begin running to lose weight. All exercise (or indeed, any movement) that we do burns calories, and since many athletes run for several miles at a time, the amount of calories burned tallies up quickly.

You will find that everyday tasks, such as carrying shopping, taking the stairs, walking from place-to-place, etc. will be made much easier after a few weeks of training. For older athletes, it can also be a good way of keeping up with your incredibly energetic and active grandchildren!

Running is a great way of meeting new people with similar interests. Joining a club or a group of runners at a park will allow you to meet many athletes of all distances, who can give you advice and help integrate you into your new hobby. The sense of belonging to a group or a club can also have big benefits such as building up your social activity and confidence. Having a training group or partner to run with can also be more motivating than running by yourself, as our competitive nature means that we don't want to get left behind!

Taking up running and setting yourself a goal (such as attaining a certain time in a race or simply completing a marathon) can give you something to focus on, and working towards this you can give yourself a sense of progression and achievement. This can also be a way to take your mind off the stresses of work or other areas of your personal life.

There will always be someone on a similar level to you throughout your running 'career' —no matter how fast or slow you can run a certain distance, you will always have somebody to run with and pit yourself against during races.

Finally, running can be one of the most inexpensive hobbies around. Although more serious athletes will want to spend money on up-to-date equipment, coaching, and even physiotherapists, the casual runner potentially only requires a pair of running shoes! Please read Chapter 2 to explore running clothing and equipment in more depth.

ii Physiological Changes

Our training is all about helping our body make adaptations to the exercise we are asking it to do. As we train, the body reacts to the challenge that it's put through and builds itself up so that it will cope better the next time that particular session occurs—this is why running a certain distance becomes easier over time! In order for this to happen, the body develops several areas and processes:

'Capillarisation'

As we exercise more, the body develops more capillaries (small blood vessels) to supply our muscles with oxygen, and grows the size of the heart muscle and efficiency of the lungs to facilitate this process. This all ends with more oxygen being available to the body and therefore more exercise can be done aerobically[1], which is the energy system that we use for endurance sport. If this process didn't happen, then we would respire anaerobically[2] and be forced to stop quickly.

Strength

Training increases our strength by building muscle to cope with the stresses of the exercise it is being asked to do. As well as the heart muscle, as described above, all muscles adapt this way and, if we do the right sort of training, get stronger to allow more efficient and more powerful movements. These improvements in our strength can then make a big difference to the speed that we can run, as well as the amount of time that that speed can be sustained.

Flexibility

Through doing a combination of running and stretching exercises away from their training sessions, runners can improve their flexibility to help safeguard from injuries and improve their technique—leading to increased performance. Runners don't have to be massively flexible, but a common problem resulting from a restricted range of movement is injury; tendons can, for example, end up stretching and getting sore because muscles can't stretch as well as they should.

Weight

When we exercise, our body burns fats (in addition to carbohydrates) that it has stored to fuel our activities. If we can reduce our body fat percentage as we train, then we will find that we can run faster with less exertion. This is because the energy we have—which is translated into movement through the above processes—will have less mass to move, and so it can move it further with the same amount of effort. There is an added bonus that reduced body fat will also mean reduced fat around your organs, which in turn decreases the risk of illness and disease—always a bonus!

It is important to note that we shouldn't go overboard with our aim to reduce body fat, as ultra-slim runners risk injury and a loss of performance, but many people new to running would benefit from reducing the amount of fat they carry.

Neuromuscular System

As we train, the body learns about what it's doing and adapts so that repeated practice makes it more efficient. There is a danger that your body will reinforce bad technique if

---

[1] Aerobic exercise is, in simple terms, low-intensity exercise that can be undertaken over a large period of time.
[2] Anaerobic exercise can only be performed in short bursts as it is very high-intensity. Improving your ability to perform exercise aerobically will therefore prevent you from burning yourself out too quickly.

you use it consistently, so it is important that we try to adopt a good technique (seen in Chapter 8) as quickly as possible.

iii Things to Consider

The beauty of running is that anyone can take it up as a hobby, and the challenge of going out and completing your runs can be a fun and educational process. There are a few things to take into account, however, before you begin training and some of these points are dealt with in more detail later on in the book:

Don't get disheartened if you find training very tough in the first few weeks. Running can be fun, but it is a physically demanding activity, so the transition from a sedentary lifestyle to an active training programme can feel tough at first.

During the first couple of weeks, it is likely that you will experience *Delayed Onset of Muscle Soreness (DOMS)*, which can basically be described as experiencing aching, stiff muscles up to three days after unfamiliar exercise. Don't worry about this—it is completely natural and it won't take long to subside as your muscles become more used to the activity you are doing.

Finally, just remember that sticking with your running and progressing in it will make you feel so much better in the long term than quitting due to a lack of motivation or finding a particular session very difficult. If you are finding it hard to keep up your will power to continue, then easing back on the workload you do can be an effective way of making training more fun, but still productive and healthy. Tips on how to adapt your training plan if necessary can be found in Chapter 6, while suggestions on how to keep motivated can be found in Chapter 13: Psychology.

Clothing and Equipment

After you've decided that you want to take up running, the next step is to make sure that you have the appropriate equipment and clothing. As said in Chapter 1, beginners can get away with only buying running shoes, but you will want to make sure that the tops, bottoms, etc. that you wear are suitable for prolonged exercise. This chapter will guide you through what type of clothing you'll want, what footwear you'll need, and will explore the usefulness of other equipment that is available for runners, such as GPS watches. Running is as expensive as you want it to be!

Chapter 2

i What Clothes do I Need?

As far as clothing goes, there is not much difference between the requirements of men and women—although the latter have the added need for a suitable sports bra. It should be noted that all items of clothing worn should ultimately be down to personal choice, and that there isn't a 'right' or 'wrong' answer to what the most suitable outfits are. Nevertheless, it is worth knowing what specialised clothing offers in comparison to standard attire, so that you know what alternatives there are if you feel uncomfortable or want a change from your current setup.

Shirts and Jerseys

The technology of clothing has advanced considerably in the past few decades, to the point that vests, shirts and tops designed specifically for the complexities of running are becoming commonplace. It should be said that 'ordinary' cotton T-Shirts are absolutely fine to wear if you already have them, but specialist running tops bring benefits such as:

- Wicking material that helps draw sweat away from your body to evaporate, instead of moisture weighing down on your top and causing chafing.
- Compression material to transport waste products away from muscles, thereby reducing the onset of fatigue.
- Reflective strips for increased safety when running at night/early morning.
- Fibres to maintain body heat, which can be useful during cold winter months.

Note that these are examples of the types of aid that specialist running clothing can bring, and that one item of clothing may not necessarily harbour all of the properties listed above. Make sure to confirm whether a piece of clothing has the benefits that you want before buying it.

Depending on the type of session that you're undertaking, you may find that you need to keep warm during a recovery or on the way to the track or the park on a cold and wet day. With that in mind, a waterproof tracksuit may be useful. As well as keeping you warm during the winter months, a waterproof tracksuit can shield you from the rain and make sure that you don't lose too much body heat as a result. It is recommended that you buy a waterproof made of breathable material, so that any perspiration that is produced while working out is expelled from your clothing.

Bottoms

The clothing requirements for the lower body of runners during exercise boils down to two choices: shorts or leggings. For many runners, it's a simple choice of shorts during the Summer and warm days, and leggings for cold Autumn/Winter periods.

Running Shorts can come in different varieties, from knee-length lycra (similar to cycling shorts) to so-called 'split' shorts which are shorter and don't cling to the body. Like most clothing, the type of running shorts that you wear is completely down to personal opinion, but each type features its own positives and negatives.

Lycra shorts are the almost-universal choice for sprinters and those who run in short bursts. This is because they are very lightweight and flexible—allowing for unhampered movement—and reduce the risk of chafing. They are also warmer than most other types of shorts during the winter due to their length and tight-fitting nature. You may find, however, that lycra shorts are too long for prolonged periods of running, and the movement of the material up and down your thigh may irritate or be uncomfortable after a few miles. In hot weather, they can also be uncomfortable and cause sweating.

Split shorts are a shorter alternative to lycra, and tend to be the shorts of choice for experienced long-distance runners. They are so called due to seam cut into the sides of the shorts that allows for freer movement. These shorts will reduce discomfort and sweating due to their very lightweight, free and minimalistic nature, so may be more ideal for sessions that will involve running for over thirty minutes. They may not be ideal for more self-conscious runners, however, as they don't cover much leg at all.

Of course, there are 'normal' nylon shorts that can be worn, if you don't feel you want or need to buy running-specific shorts. Bear in mind though that the length and looseness of these shorts may hinder your range of movement, and that their flapping around may be irritating or uncomfortable if you set out on a long, several-mile run.

There are a couple of general points to think about when buying shorts, whichever type they may be. The first is to make sure that they are made from a lightweight, breathable wicking material, as (like shirts/jerseys mentioned earlier in the chapter) these prevent sweat from absorbing into your clothing and weighing you down, and help minimise chafing. Secondly, although there exist unisex shorts, it is much more beneficial to buy some specifically for your gender, as they are constructed to fit the different body structures of men and women (e. g. some men's shorts feature inner briefs).

Running Leggings (sometimes referred to as 'tights') are an ideal alternative to shorts for those cold autumn and winter months. Tracksuit bottoms are also designed to keep you warm during cold days, but they tend to be too baggy to mobilise properly, and any moisture they take on tends to be absorbed—which eventually results in them weighing you down and making runs that much harder. Leggings therefore were introduced to both keep athletes warm, and to allow the full range of movement that comes with wearing shorts.

The features of running tights that you should look out for are much the same as those of running shorts—i. e. lightweight, wicking material to prevent absorption of moisture first and foremost. There is also the option of buying 'compression' tights, which hold your legs tightly and help reduce injury risk, as well as assist in speeding up recovery.

Socks

Yes, there are even special socks for running! It should be said that regular socks are absolutely fine to wear, and that you won't be putting yourself at a disadvantage if you wear them, but there are different types of socks out there for runners, each serving a different purpose.

Socklets—these only come up as high as the ankle bone and fit inside your trainer for comfort.

Anti-Blister Socks—these socks have two layers of material to prevent rubbing.

9

Compression Socks—these hold the muscles of the calf tight and therefore help increase circulation and reduce risk of injury.

The choice of sock is up to the individual—the above socks tend to be more expensive than regular ones (especially compression socks) so bear that in mind. If you have a history of calf strains, however, then compression socks are a good choice to give you long-term support in that area of weakness.

Underwear and Sports Bras

Finally, we come to the clothing that we wear underneath our shirts and shorts—which is just as important!

Ideally, underwear for runners should be comfortable and made from a material that isn't going to cause chafing once you start to sweat. Keeping in with the general theme throughout this section, soft materials with a good wicking capacity would be the best choice, as the most common cause of chafing is moisture between your skin and clothing material. It may still be worth applying Vaseline to vulnerable areas though as, sometimes, suitable underwear unfortunately doesn't stop chafing around the insides of your legs.

One final consideration for underwear is keeping warm in the winter, so thermal underwear as (or just over) your base layer may be something that you would want to invest in.

For female runners, there is the extra requirement of a suitable sports bra. Unfortunately, many women turn away from high-impact sports because of a lack of breast support, which can make activities such as running uncomfortable and even cause back or chest pain due to excess movement.

The main points to think about when buying a sports bra are:

- Does it give suitable support?
- Does the stitching cause chafing?
- Does it have fastenings that rub against the skin?

You will need to try and buy a sports bra that is supportive to your shape, but not restrictive. It should be comfortable to wear, and there should be minimal movement when you jump—if this is the case, then the action of running won't have too much impact on your body. As well as this, try to make sure that the areas that touch the skin have as little in the way of stitching and fasteners as possible, as this will greatly minimise any discomfort felt whilst wearing the bra.

ii What Running Shoes Should I Wear?

Perhaps the most difficult choice, and the one that should require the most thought—after all, these will be your main tool during training in your quest to achieve your goals! There is a massive range of options—with shoes of all shapes, sizes, surfaces, weights, etc. on offer— so the advice we give is aimed at narrowing down the sort of footwear that you're looking for. Shops will allow you to try on shoes and maybe use a treadmill/jog around the store while wearing them, so make sure that you make the most of this opportunity to try different types and find exactly what you're looking for.

Nevertheless, you should ask yourself a few questions before you set about looking for running shoes, so that you can have an idea of a starting point to work from:

What Size Shoes do I Need?

Bear in mind that feet tend to swell after running a few miles, as well as the fact that supposedly identical shoe sizes can differ depending on footwear and manufacturer, so getting half a size larger than normal everyday footwear may be a good idea.

How Much do I Weigh?

A large force (which can sometimes be several times your body weight) is put through your running shoe on each stride, so you will need to ensure that they can cope with the impact. Some shoes are designed specifically for heavier runners by providing extra cushioning.

What Surface do I Usually Run on?

This typically falls into one of three categories—each type of shoe has soles designed to cope with the different surfaces that they encounter.

Road Running shoes have a shallow tread on the sole, which is designed to be long-lasting. The more lightweight versions—with relatively little heel support—are known as 'Racing Flats', and are recommended for more experienced, lighter runners who have outgrown general, all-purpose running shoes and want something more specialised. Road Running shoes and Racing Flats are good for running on synthetic athletics tracks too.

On- and off-road Running shoes are suitable for both roads (or general tarmac surfaces) and footpaths made from gravel, dirt, etc. These shoes have a deeper tread to cope with uneven surfaces.

Finally, purely *Off-Road Running* shoes are available, which focus chiefly on grip—you will need lots of traction for the muddy, uneven, slippery surfaces that you will endure during cross-country and trail runs.

Do I Overpronate, Underpronate or am I a Neutral Runner?

If this sentence looks like gibberish to you, then don't worry—it only refers to the position that your foot naturally lands. This affects the type of shoe that is suitable for an individual, and is arguably the most important consideration.

Shops will have experts that can watch you run and evaluate what 'type' of runner you are, but you can also get a good idea of whether you over/underpronate by examining your footprint when your feet are wet—for example after a shower.

Underpronators ('supinator') will have a footprint like this. This print will leave a very thin band on the outside of the foot, if any at all, between the heel and forefoot. Most underpronators run primarily on their forefoot, and their running style may increase stress on this area of the foot—therefore requiring a lot of cushioning. If you are an underpronator, then we would advise avoiding motion control or structured shoes that are designed to reduce foot mobility.

If your footprint looks like this, then you are a 'neutral' runner. A normal foot plant usually leaves around half of the footprint (namely the outside part). When running you land on the outside of the heel and roll inwards slightly to absorb shock while moving off the big toe. The recommended footwear is a 'Stability' shoe, as these offer a good blend of cushioning, durability and features that control the rotation of the foot on landing.

Finally, you are an overpronator if your footprint looks like this. This print leaves the whole of the foot because the arch collapses through the foot motion—the foot strikes at the heel and moves inwards excessively. Overpronators without corrective footwear are much more likely to get injuries when running—especially in the knee and hip areas. We would highly recommend shoes with Motion Control characteristics, which are designed to strongly limit the inward rolling of the foot and are useful for medium-to-severe overpronators who need maximum support.

Do I Run a Lot of Miles or Relatively Few?

Generally speaking, the more mileage you do, the more you should spend on your running shoes. Doing several dozen miles a week will put a fair amount of strain on your legs, so more expensive, better-quality shoes will be useful to cushion the blow on each stride. Equally, if you have poor technique then better shoes will help counter this more than cheaper ones.

One tip to reduce the price you pay but still have quality gear is to ask for last year's model—often, the price of these are significantly reduced while being almost exactly the same as this year's, much-more-expensive shoes.

When Should I Replace my Trainers?

You may already have shoes but want to know when the time is right to look for a new pair. Trainers lose their cushioning after 300-600 miles of running, so replacing them after running this distance is the best way to avoid impact injuries. Once you see that the heels have worn down and the grip is coming away, then your shoes will need to be changed.

iii What Other Equipment Will I Need?

Firstly, we should say that no-one *needs* the following equipment, but they can be useful tools for runners to make training easier. We haven't included things like sunglasses, bags, etc. as these aren't particularly specific or vital to running, but by all means buy them if you wish!

GPS Watches

These are becoming more popular, as they can tell you how far you've run, for how long (it is a watch!), your average speed, and even your altitude and heart-rate. This can be very beneficial both during a session, as you can judge and adjust your pace according to your target time/speed, and after the session, as you can evaluate how you've done in comparison to other sessions and keep a log of your progression. One disadvantage is that a GPS Watch can be expensive, but as it can do the job of a stopwatch, pedometer, heart rate monitor and satnav (to a degree), it can be a useful purchase.

Pedometers

These can serve as a cheap alternative to GPS watches (though you would need a stopwatch too!), as they work out roughly how far you have travelled and can work under the cover of trees or other areas where GPS watches may struggle to receive a signal.

Heart Rate Monitors

Long distance runners may want some sessions to take place without their heart rate going above a certain point, and these can help with that as well as work out your maximum heart rate during exercise. They can also be used to find out whether you have an illness on the way and should rest instead of train, as an elevated heart rate is usually the sign of an infection or virus.

Summary

✓ *There are many items of specialist clothing now available to runners. None of it is 'vital' per se, but the wicking qualities that many tops and bottoms have will make running that little bit more pleasant and comfortable.*

✓ *Buying the correct type of running shoe is important. Evaluating how often you will use them, how far you will run each week, and the surface that you will be running on is important when deciding what to buy and how much to spend. Ask shop assistants for advice if you're stuck.*

✓ *GPS Watches and other gadgets can make it easier to track your heart rate, average pace, overall time, etc. If they are not too expensive, then they are a useful acquisition and will give you more information to work with if you need to evaluate your training and your physical condition.*

Chapter 3

Planning your Training

So, you've bought some running shoes, all the clothes you'll need for the year, and you are fully committed to getting fitter and healthier through your running training. The next step is actually figuring out how you'll be achieving the goals you set for yourself. This can seem like a daunting prospect, and may feel like it'll require lots of hard work, but even a little bit of rough planning before embarking upon a training regime can be the difference between achieving your goals and being left disappointed after a few months. It is worth putting aside a fair bit of time to plan before you start your training as this will give you a guideline to follow during the first few uncertain weeks, and after this original point you will only need to tweak your ideas to suit/improve your training.

i What can I do to Start Planning my Training?

Before you start your training schedule, you will need to decide what you want to achieve from your running (e. g. weight loss, a certain time for 10k, etc.), the resources that you have to achieve that, and your current situation in terms of fitness and speed. An ideal way to do this is to ask yourself a series of questions, including but not limited to:

- What distance will I concentrate on?
- How fast can I run at the moment?
- Are there any races I want to compete in, and will I use these to monitor my progress?
- How old am I?
- How much time can I dedicate to training?
- Do I have any health-related problems that may restrict my training?
- What time can I realistically aim for in 5k/10k/half-marathon? Will this be in a one-off race or do I want to back it up with several similar performances?

Once you have answers to these questions, then you can start creating a more thorough plan of action for the first few weeks. Remember that it is very unlikely that the plan will immediately be perfect, and the first week may reveal that you were too ambitious/too cautious with your starting point, but tweaking and perfecting your plan to become more appropriate will become much easier with practice. Ideas and guidance on what to do for the first week will be explored in more detail in Chapter 4.

ii How do I Build a Training Plan?

Normally, you or your coach would create a multi-layered training plan, the broadest layer of which would involve separating a year's worth of training into distinct 'phases', in which you can focus on different aspects of your running. The year is commonly known in coaching circles as a *macrocycle*—we wouldn't advise worrying about the technical terms, and certainly not this one as we will be concentrating on the first few months of your running career.

What we will be concentrating on are the two other, smaller parts of a training programme—the monthly breakdown of what you are going to concentrate on, and the individual sessions themselves. This section won't include specific examples of training sessions (those can be found in Chapter 4), but will give some general 'rules' to follow.

First of all, you should plan roughly what intensity you will want each week to be during each one month period. As a beginner, we would suggest that your first week be very low intensity—three or four light sessions would be a good starting point—with a gradual build up thereafter for the next three weeks. Once you have familiarised yourself with a training routine, then you should be ready to vary the effort levels of each week without worrying about injuring yourself by overexerting your body. Momentum Sports tends to use the following schedule for its athletes:

Week 1: High/Hard Intensity
Week 2: Normal Intensity
Week 3: High/Hard Intensity
Week 4: Low/Easy Intensity

The workload of each week is up to the individual, but an example of what each one can entail would be:

High/Hard Intensity – 5 sessions per week; 2 easy, 1 medium and 2 hard
Normal Intensity – 4 sessions per week; 2 easy, 1 medium and 1 hard
Low/Easy Intensity – 3 sessions per week; 2 easy, 1 medium

[Note: this amount of sessions per week should be something to aspire to after a few months rather than start with immediately. For the first few weeks, fewer sessions per week would be recommended, with more sessions added after your body has had time to adapt to the new training programme.]

This is pretty simplistic, but should give you a basic understanding of how to vary your training schedule to allow yourself enough rest and recovery, whilst still feeling that you're working hard. You could have the same number of sessions each week, but alter the speed that you run at and the recovery between each run (if you're doing an interval session) according to which week you are currently on. Equally, you could have a certain type of training session only occurring on 'Hard' or 'Easy' weeks.

On top of this, we would highly recommend planning to spend some time on improving your strength with circuit training, and maintaining or improving your mobility through stretches and drills. Again, the intensity of these sessions should vary depending on what type of week it is, and you could choose only to perform them during medium and high intensity periods, but making sure you include strength and mobility work as well as running will help you achieve the best results you possibly can. Advice on individual exercises for strength and mobility can be found in Chapter 16 and Chapter 7 respectively.

One very important thing to stress is that the importance of 'easy' weeks shouldn't be underestimated. Understandably, dedicating one week to (mostly) resting and relaxing may not seem like the best way to get yourself into shape or improve your times, but not allowing yourself to recuperate properly after a tiring week can have an adverse effect on your energy levels and therefore your ability to train at your highest level.

Another important thing to note is that you should allow yourself to be flexible. There may well be a time in which you run into a heavy period at work or catch an illness, and at these times cramming in the training that you planned for yourself may not be the best plan. Instead, missing a session or two, evaluating what you had to miss, and sensibly shuffling your upcoming sessions to ensure that you complete the most important ones would be preferable.

iii What Sort of Goals can I Set Myself?

Setting distinct objectives before you start your running schedule is important as they enable you to bring some sort of structure to your training, and allow your progression to be measureable. This is vital for a well-structured training regime, as it makes editing and adapting your plans to improve your weaknesses far easier. It can also serve as a useful indicator of what you can expect to achieve in upcoming races (as well as whether or not you're likely to run a Personal Best).

What these targets/objectives are is completely up to the individual. Some runners may want to lose 5kgs over the course of a 3-month plan, whereas others may want their objective for a 12-month season to be achieving 50 minutes for 10k. A common acronym that is used in terms of making your goals as useful as possible is SMARTER. This stands for:

S   goals should be *specific*. For example 'I will run 50:00 for 10k' rather than 'I will enjoy my running'.

M   these targets should be *measureable*. This is easy enough, as weight-based objectives can easily be measured, as can training times.

A   goals should be *adjustable*, so that you can easily change your objective should you progress quicker/slower than expected at the beginning of your training.

R   targets need to be *realistic*. Obviously you will want to challenge yourself, but make sure that your objective is possible to achieve. Aiming for sub-11 seconds for 100m if you're over 40 may not be the best idea!

T   you should set a *time* frame to achieve your goal. There are no rules for this, but you will want to set a point at which you can evaluate whether or not you succeeded in achieving your objective.

E   goals should be challenging and *exciting*. This can be seen to work in tandem with 'realistic' – don't make targets so easy that can be achieved within a week!

R   lastly, goals should be *recorded*,

If you can meet the criteria laid out above when setting your objectives at the start of your training schedule, and if you spend a while laying out your training plan before you begin—including breaking it up into distinct periods of general training, event-specific training, and preparing for competition, then success will become that much easier to achieve.

Summary

✓   *Set out what your goals are before planning your training, as this will give you a direction to aim toward rather than improvising and suffering a disjointed first couple of weeks.*

✓   *Make sure that you incorporate a mixture of 'easy', 'hard' and 'normal' weeks into your training schedule. This will ensure that you give yourself enough variety in your training to prevent it from becoming stale and boring, and will make sure that you don't overtrain.*

✓   *It is important for you to set goals to give your training purpose. Make sure that your goals are specific and easy to evaluate, so that you can determine exactly how successful they were and make changes/further goals for the future.*

The First Week

Hopefully you will have taken some of the advice on board from Chapter 3, and know what your goals are, when you hope to achieve them by, and when your competition period occurs (if you have one). As everyone reading this book will have different goals and different levels of fitness, it would be impossible to produce an all-encompassing plan for the first week that everyone should follow. Instead we will use this Chapter to give you some solid tips and suggestions on how to begin your training, as well as the types of individual sessions that you can use to experiment with in the first couple of weeks.

i What Should Happen During my First Week of Training?

The first bit of advice is that you should not be alarmed if the first week of your training doesn't go to plan and you feel more tired/ache more than you expected. For many, including those who have played other sports regularly, the first week of running training will be the first time that they have really got to grips with long periods of concentrated running, and even light sessions may be hard work. It should not, however, necessarily be seen as representative of your training schedule as a whole. Over time, with the physiological changes that will occur described in Chapter 1, your body will get accustomed to the feel of running, and you will become more aware of what routines/sessions work best for you, so you will find that the uncertainty of the first week will be forgotten about as the days go on.

In fact, the best course of action for the first week is to not push yourself much at all! Your training in the first week should ideally be light and relaxed, with plenty of time to recover from any running that you do, so as to not push your body to levels that it may not at all be used to. If you are coming into running from another sport, or you already had another hobby such as cycling or swimming, then these are useful activities that you can also do during the first week to keep up your fitness.

ii What Sorts of Sessions can I do?

Arguably the most important part of setting yourself training is knowing what you're actually going to do in individual sessions! Of course, there is always the option of choosing to run three miles and then increasing the distance by one mile each week—but this would not be a very exciting routine and would only work on one aspect of your running (namely aerobic endurance). It would be much more interesting and beneficial to include a bit of variety into your training schedule—for those who are fairly new to running, doing a mixture of the following sessions should be enough to give you good all-round conditioning during the first few weeks:

Walking

Walking may not seem to be the most obvious choice of session for a runner, but it has a number of benefits for those starting their training. For one, it isn't as strenuous as running, so you won't feel as drained at the end of your session, and the amount of calories that walking burns isn't too far behind that of running—as long as you keep up a decent strolling pace. Choosing to do some walking sessions during your first week would be a good choice in keeping yourself active without causing much fatigue.

Gentle Fartlek Sessions

Fartlek sessions involve running a set distance, but splitting the run into parts of varying speeds. For example, an inexperienced runner might decide to do a one-mile run, and alternate running at 8-minute mile pace and 11-minute mile pace every quarter of a mile. It can be also be done by time, e. g. alternate between speeds every 30 seconds. You could try something like this for the first week, but alternate between walking and jogging. Covering a maximum distance of only a couple of miles would be fine and give you a good introduction to extended periods of training, without the stresses of immediately running several miles.

Long Slow Run

After having experimented with the gentle sessions, you may wish to give a long run a go. This is the most common form of training for newcomers to long-distance events, and it does have its merits through improving your endurance and helping you get used to prolonged stints of running. For experienced athletes, these runs are usually 1½ - 2½ hours long and involve running at a slow pace that keeps your heart rate under 140bpm (this is known as an 'aerobic' session). For beginners, however, 1½ - 2½ hour sessions should not be considered until you are at least 6 months into your training. For the first few weeks, runs of 20-30 minutes are a good starting point if easily achievable.

Note that it would be better to perform this sort of session on grass/softer surfaces rather than on tarmac. Running on roads and pavements tends to put more pressure on your ankles and shins, so absolute beginners may find that concrete should be avoided until they have sufficient strength in their feet/legs.

Interval Sessions

In basic terms, this type of session involves several repetitions of a certain distance, with recoveries between each run. The distance of each repetition, effort required for each run, and the amount of time needed for recovery will differ from person to person, but they are generally designed to be high-intensity, high-quality sessions.

Interval runs are very useful in improving your overall speed. As the total distance covered throughout a session is split up into several parts, you can run at a faster pace than you would during a long, steady run. This can be useful in getting used to the feeling of running at or faster than 'race pace'—i.e. the sort of speed you would want to run during a race, or a speed fast enough to achieve a personal best—and getting used to the feeling of running at that speed.

A recommended starting point for beginners of long distance running would be to four repetitions of 1000m, with three minutes' recovery in between each. The speed at which you run can be experimented with after you have performed this type of session several times, as can the amount of repetitions, distance, and the amount of recovery.

[Note: Recoveries, as a guide, should be long enough to allow your heart rate to drop to 100-110 bpm. During your first interval session, you can either alter the speed of your run to enable your heart rate to drop to this point within 3 minutes, or simply increase the recovery time until this heart rate is reached and you feel able to run again.]

Recovery/Easy Runs

These runs should be as they sound—a slow, steady run simply for maintaining fitness and flushing out waste products/stiffness after a hard week of training. It is important that you have enough of these sessions in your schedule: it is always tempting to do as much training as possible to get fitter and faster, but there is only so much work that our bodies can do before we become too tired to perform a worthwhile session and risk injury. Fitting in one of these sessions a week should be an ideal way to get started and to go into the next week of training in good stead.

Summary

✓ *For the first week, very light training sessions are the way to go to familiarise your body with the rigours of running.*

✓ *There are various sessions that you can choose that will work on strengthening different functions of the body. Walking/steady runs are good to improve stamina and to work your body without inducing too much fatigue, while fartlek and interval runs can help improve your speed. Finally, recovery runs are there to help your body recuperate after difficult sessions.*

The First Month

With any luck, the first week will have been a successful one and you are feeling excited about where your running programme will take you. Of course, a training regime lasts longer than one week, so you will want to know how to continue your running! This chapter will give you tips on how to expand the work you did in the first week into something more long-term, as well as activities you can do to evaluate your capabilities.

i What Should Happen During the First Month?

You will have completed a whole week of training now, albeit (ideally) at a level that is some way below your best to make sure that you don't injure yourself or tire yourself out too much. The serious stuff can now begin!

We do, however, recommend that you build gradually and never ramp up the mileage or intensity too much too soon; in order to make sure this principle is kept, we would recommend you adopt the 10% rule. This means that the mileage in any normal training week is never 10% more than the previous normal week, so if the aggregate mileage of all your sessions during Week 1 was 20 miles, make sure that Week 2 does not exceed 22. Though you may be tempted to boost the mileage quickly, especially if the first week was very enjoyable and easy, you will risk injury and fatigue if you take a step too far for your body to cope.

There is an exception to this rule—if you have an easy week in which you significantly reduce the mileage from the norm, then this should not factor into the 10% rule. For example, if your mileage progression over a 4-week period is 20, 22, 24, 10, then clearly we wouldn't want Week 5 to involve only 11 miles!

A good way to keep a record of how you performed is to create a training diary. Whether this is an actual diary or simply a spreadsheet is up to you, but noting down the distance of each run during the session, the target time if you have one[3], the recovery between runs, and your actual time will give you a good basis to work on to develop your training. There is also a fifth aspect that you can record: the session's difficulty. Evaluating the difficulty of a session with a mark out of 10—1 for very, very easy and 10 indicating a very hard, almost-impossible session—can make future planning of sessions much easier.

If you failed to make your target times in a session and rated it 10 for difficulty, then you should probably look at making any targets you have easier, giving yourself more recovery, or shortening the distance of each run slightly. If you want to cover the same distance, then you could shorten the distance of every run and add an extra one—e. g. 4 x 500m becomes 5 x 400m. More examples of adjustments you can make to your training schedule can be found in Chapter 6, Part i.

Finally, don't get too disheartened if the euphoria of your first week wears off quickly. It should be emphasised that running is not an easy hobby, and a lot of hard work will have to be put in to achieve your goals and get stronger and fitter. However, it should never get to the stage where you dread going out for a training session—we don't mean nervousness or concern that a particular session will be hard or tiring, but rather a lack of motivation or saying to yourself 'I don't want to run but I guess I have to'. Running should be enjoyable, and you should feel like to *want* to do it rather than feel obliged to,

---

[3] If you are a beginner and are not sure what constitutes a 'sensible' target time for your distance, then it may be better not to set one for the first couple of sessions. Although setting targets is a good thing, it would be better to wait until you've run a specific distance a few times – without the pressure of beating a target— rather than set an unrealistic aim and become disappointed if you fail to make it.

so you will need to make sure that you keep it varied, make sessions easier if you're feeling fatigued, or make them harder to give yourself a challenge. A great way of keeping yourself motivated is to make your running a social activity—if possible, get a friend or two to join in or help you with your sessions, or look to clubs in the local area for the possibility of meeting and befriending other runners of a similar standard.

ii Running Tests

Another way of keeping your interest going during the first month of your training is to set yourself a few benchmarks through various running tests. As your training programme progresses, it would be useful to discover exactly which areas need improvement so that you can adapt your training to work on these. As well as entering races every so often to see how you're getting on (see Chapter 6, Part iii), there are a number of these tests—both well-known and Momentum Sports' own—that you can use to evaluate specific areas of your running. Performing these every few months can tell you how far you are progressing in each area, and whether you need to change your training schedule to make improvements.

Testing Your Speed

Now, if you will be doing dozens of miles per week, and no shorter than a mile in any given session, then a test of your maximum speed may seem pointless. It is, however, useful for any runner to know what their top speed is, and improving how fast you can run will mean that slower speeds are far easier to maintain, which can make a huge difference in any event—long-distance or otherwise. In simpler terms, if your top speed is 10mph, then running at 7mph is 70% of your top speed and therefore your effort level. If you can increase your top speed to 14mph, then 7mph becomes only 50% of your maximum capability, and in turn each stride will require less effort. That pace will therefore become easier to sustain over the course of a long run, which will allow you to save more energy for faster bursts of speed as you come towards the end of the course.

[Note: Before attempting this test, it is very important that you are fully warmed up as this kind of explosive activity will be alien to almost anyone. It will certainly be too strenuous for anybody to attempt without preparing their body sufficiently first—check Chapter 7 for advice on what to include in your warm up routine. We would also advise having become accustomed to training for a few weeks before doing the speed test.]

This test is designed to discover how fast you can run when you're travelling at full speed, so we want to remove the element of acceleration. Therefore, we suggest that the following would be a good indicator of top speed:

   3 x 30m flying, with a full recovery

This means taking 20m or so to build up to top speed, and then timing over a duration of 30m. It can be quite difficult to get an accurate measurement of this, but having a dedicated 'timer' and someone dropping their arm when the 'start line' is breached will help you achieve a good degree of accuracy. Furthermore, performing the test 3 times and taking the average should give you a fairly accurate indication of what your top speed is.

Generally, a time of 5 seconds would be very good for a long-distance runner. In any case, the time achieved during the first test may not be that significant, but further tests every few months will tell you how you're progressing and by how much you've improved your speed.

Testing Your Lactic Tolerance

Lactate is a by-product of running at a speed which is higher than your body can power purely from the oxygenated blood in your system. This produces an acid which, when present in enough quantities, will stop your continued running (as a defence mechanism against your headstrong determination damaging your body). It is useful to test how well you can cope running with elevated lactate levels, which can be done as follow:

1. Run as far as possible in 30 seconds and work out what distance you ran.
2. Take a full recovery—20 minutes should be enough.
3. Run a 600m time trial as fast as possible.
4. Calculate the time per 100m for each of the runs[4] and take the difference.

For long-distance runners, a difference below 3 seconds would be a very good 'score'. Again, you may wish to wait until the test has been completed a second time before evaluating if your lactic tolerance is something to be worked on, but generally, the smaller the difference between the time per 100m of the two runs, the better your lactic tolerance.

Testing Your Aerobic Capacity

There are a few options for testing your aerobic capacity—in simple terms, this means testing your body's endurance.

Half Marathons/Marathons. A simple way of evaluating your aerobic endurance is your time taken to run a half marathon or marathon.

Cooper Test. Another accurate but easy way of measuring your aerobic capacity is to perform the standard Cooper Test, which involves running as far as possible in 12 minutes[5]. The distance after the time has elapsed is then taken as an indicator of your endurance capabilities. An example for this test is given in Table 5.1.

---

[4] To work out the time per 100m for the first run, divide 30 by the distance covered, and then multiply by 100. For the second run, divide the overall time in seconds by 6
[5] Cooper, Kenneth H. (1969), *Aerobics*, Bantam Books

iii What are Some More Advanced Training Sessions That I can do?

The session types in the previous chapter will give you a good grounding to your training, but after a couple of weeks you may want to start to take it up a notch. Below is a brief overview of some more advanced sessions that you can try.

Age		Very Good	Good	Average	Poor	Very Poor
17-20	M	3000+m	2700-3000m	2500-2699m	2300-2499m	2300-m
	F	2300+m	2100-2300m	1800-2099m	1700-1799m	1700-m
20-29	M	2800+m	2400-2800m	2200-2399m	1600-2199m	1600-m
	F	2700+m	2200-2700m	1800-2199m	1500-1799m	1500-m
30-39	M	2700+m	2300-2700m	1900-2299m	1500-1899m	1500-m
	F	2500+m	2000-2500m	1700-1999m	1400-1699m	1400-m
40-49	M	2500+m	2100-2500m	1700-2099m	1400-1699m	1400-m
	F	2300+m	1900-2300m	1500-1899m	1200-1499m	1200-m
50+	M	2400+m	2000-2400m	1600-1999m	1300-1599m	1300-m
	F	2200+m	1700-2200m	1400-1699m	1100-1399m	1100-m

Table 5.1
The Cooper Test

As with all of your sessions during the first month, if you find any of these very difficult then don't be ashamed to ease back a lot, or revert back to the gentle sessions again for a few weeks. Slow, steady, safe progression is always preferable to hasty progression that increases the risk of injuring yourself!

Pyramids

These sessions take on a similar format to interval training, in that several runs are completed during a session with a rest in-between. However, with pyramids there is a change in the distance of repetitions as the session progresses—whether shorter, longer or fluctuating between the two is up to the individual. This means that a large range of distances, and therefore speeds, can be experienced during a single session.

These sessions are a popular choice for coaches as the speed and recovery elements allow for an athlete to experiment with different phases of their races, or to simply practice running at different speeds. For example, a 1500m runner may do a session of 800m, 600m, 300m—in which the first repetition is aimed at running conservatively as they would during a the first two laps of a 1500m race, the 600m practices fast but relaxed running like the middle phase of a middle distance race, and the 300m is for the sprint at the end. The athlete would be able to complete each run in a faster time than they would during a continuous race, and so they are able to 'overload' and acclimatise their body to running at speeds that wouldn't otherwise be achieved if they were to only practice 1500m and above.

Speed Work

This could be seen as a variation on the interval session (page 21), but with a much bigger emphasis on running faster than race pace or Personal Best (PB) pace by shortening the repetition distance even more. These sessions will teach the body to cope with higher-paced running, with the view that 'normal' or 'race pace' running will gradually seem easier in comparison.

Similarly to the interval sessions, the requirements and recommendations for speed work sessions will vary depending on the individual, but a good starting point would be 5-6 repetitions of 400m, with 3 minutes' recovery, running around 2 seconds quicker per 100m than your chosen 'race pace'.

Tempo Runs

This is typically a session that involves one hard and continuous run, usually performed at around 80-90% of your flat-out speed. The run can be of any length, but at no point should you feel that you're too tired to continue—one simple but accurate way to tell if you're running at the correct speed is to carry on a normal conversation (if you're running with a partner), or being able to say a sentence aloud without pausing for breath.

Summary

✓   *Remember the 10% rule. Apart from the times that you will cut the mileage for easy weeks, make sure that you never cover more than 110% of the distance of the previous week. Doing this will prevent any burnout and reduce the risk of injury through overexertion.*

✓   *Running tests can be a good way of monitoring your progress and evaluating your strengths and weaknesses. Doing them once every few months can reveal whether or not your training has been developing the areas you want to improve.*

✓   *After a gentle first week, introducing intervals, tempo runs, pyramids and speed work will further strengthen the various important aspects of running: fitness, endurance and speed.*

Adapting Your Training Plan

As Chapter 3 discussed, spending a bit of time planning before you embark upon a training schedule will benefit you in the long run, as you will have a specific, dedicated path to follow as opposed to randomly choosing distances and speeds to run. It would be impossible to prepare for every scenario, however, and there will almost certainly come a point in which you feel that you have to make adjustments to your training plan. This could be for a number of reasons, such as fatigue, finding training too easy, or simply wanting to make a change or inject a bit of variety into your routine each week.

i What Alterations can I Make to my Training Plan?

If you feel that your training schedule is in need of a change, first you will need to identify what you feel is 'wrong' about your current routine. Below is a list of possible problems and suggested solutions, but note that each one may simply be an isolated incident—it only becomes a cause for concern after two or three occurrences in succession:

I'm Getting Very Tired and Unable to Complete Sessions

There is no shame in making each training session easier. Simply cut down the distance that you cover or the speed that you run, and gradually build this little by little each week. This will be much more beneficial to your confidence and energy levels than launching yourself straight into fast, hard sessions.

I'm too Tired to Motivate Myself for Sessions

The problem here may be a lack of an 'easy' week. When we are trying to get ourselves into shape, the most tempting thing to do is push ourselves constantly. Dedicating at least one week per month to cutting down on mileage and the number of sessions per week will help you recover sufficiently—allowing you to be as fresh as possible for the tough sessions when they do come around.

Training is too Easy

As Chapter 5 stated, if this is the case, what you don't want to do is suddenly increase your mileage so much that you tire yourself out for several days due to your body not being used to the workload. The best short-term solution is to make your target times, or the pace that you run at, faster, and build up the mileage gradually each week—generally, no more than 110% of the previous week each time.

I'm Bored of Long Runs/Tempo Runs/Interval Sessions

If you are only doing one type of session or doing one type much more frequently than others, then the lack of variety may start to grate. Introducing different types of sessions (see Chapters 5 and 6 for examples) allows you to work on more areas of training (speed, endurance, lactic tolerance, etc), and therefore make useful all-round improvements.

I've Decided to Enter a Race and Don't Know how to Prepare

The topic of races will be explored below, but generally training doesn't have to change until seven days prior to the race. The week leading up to it should be high-quality work at (or a touch faster than) race pace, with the final two or three days before the competition as rest days—though you may want to perform a gentle jog or warm up to keep yourself supple during this time.

ii Entering Races

[Note: this section discusses what races are on offer and why we choose to compete. For detailed advice on what you should do before races, how to taper, how to prepare, etc. then please read Chapter 15.]

One of the best ways of evaluating your progress and seeing if you've got stronger is to enter a race every now and again (if you want to be a more serious runner, then this could go up to one race a week during the competition phase of training!). To get as good an idea as possible of how well you've progressed (if at all), then entering two or more races of the same distance would be best—comparing a 5k run to a half marathon would be very difficult due to the different tactics and target paces utilised in those events.

Some cross-country event organisers will put on a series of races, in which a route will be used several times over the course of a few months—this would be even better for getting a fair comparison between two results. Though two races over 5k would (obviously) cover the same distance, each course has its own amount of uphill/downhill sections—as well as differing gradients of hills—so you may find that your time for Course A is much better than your time for Course B mostly because of a particularly tough section in the latter. Though you would still be able to draw conclusions and make comparisons from two different courses (for example, only being a few seconds off your PB in the tough Course B would tell you that you are progressing well), using the same one twice will ensure that the challenge was identical. Any differences in the result could be put down to tiredness, being stronger, feeling under the weather, pacing yourself better, etc.

There are a variety of races that you can do as part of your training or during the competition season, and below we have listed some common types of events that are good for newcomers and experienced runners alike. Some of them can be entered by anyone, some of them need to be registered for, and some would require you to be a member of an athletics club, but all of them are suitable for somebody wanting to test themselves in an official competition:

Park Runs

For: Anyone. Some races require prior registration (www.parkrun.com)

Throughout the whole country, park runs are held every week—usually on Saturdays and Sundays. The typical distance of a park run is 5k, though this isn't always the case so make sure to check before you turn up. The terrain of these races can vary, too—some courses may be hilly or take place partly on grass, partly on tarmac, etc.

As they are the most accessible races, and can feature several hundred participants at a time, there are a whole variety of standards at each event, so you won't have to worry about being left behind. Some organisers also arrange post-race social meetings, so it can be a great way to find training partners and make friends with similar hobbies.

Road Races

For: Anyone who has registered

For the purpose of this section, 'Road Races' refer to casual races, of a similar length to park runs, that take place solely on road/pavement surfaces. The terrain in these races is almost completely even underfoot (there may be potholes here and there), so they may suit newcomers or runners not used to uneven surfaces more than park runs would. There is also a great atmosphere at these casual events, as many people use them to raise money for charity, and there are sometimes prizes, T-Shirts and other memorabilia for all competitors.

One disadvantage, however, is that the relentlessly hard surface can cause discomfort in those without sufficient strength in their legs, and this is a common cause of shin splints (see Chapter 17). If you are planning to take part in a road race, then it would be advisable to spend a few sessions training on hard surfaces in order to get your body accustomed to the demands of the terrain.

Off-Road Races
For: Anyone who has registered

Though Park Runs are technically off-road races, here we are referring to 'fell' or 'trail' races, which often take place over mountainous, or at least very hilly, terrain. These races tend to concentrate more on navigation through difficult landscapes rather than pure speed, so these probably aren't the best races to choose if you want to improve your technique or get a good time in a certain distance! They are, however, a fun experience and can give you some good practice of hill running, which is often required as part of more 'conventional' races such as park runs. As they often cover several kilometres at a time, too, they are useful races for improving your endurance and overall fitness.

Half Marathons and Marathons
For: Successful applicants. Some races (usually the most popular ones) require a qualifying standard to guarantee entry or strengthen applications

At 13. 1 miles and 26. 2 miles in length respectively, half marathons and marathons are often the big season's target for runners, who use shorter park/road races as part of their training in the quest to get as fit as possible for the main event. These races are obviously hard work, but the sense of achievement, the buoyant atmosphere, and feeling of togetherness with your fellow competitors make half marathons and marathons a worthwhile and rewarding venture for all runners!

Track Open Meets
For: Anyone

These races take place on standard 400m tracks, and distances can range from short 100m sprints to 5000m (10000m is also a possibility, but this is fairly rare). Open meets tend to group athletes according to their best times, though some of the longer distance events will have everyone running together. Regardless, with the accessibility of Open meets, they often attract athletes of all abilities, so you should find that you will have at least one person of a similar standard to pit yourself against! Though doing 12 and a half laps of a track can get monotonous, you are at least guaranteed a flat and consistent course, so this sort of race can be good to use to monitor your progress every few weeks/month.

Club Track Meets

For: Those picked to represent a club (The act and benefits of joining clubs are discussed in Chapter 18, Part ii.)

Track meets for athletics clubs can take many guises, from local competitions that are (generally) relaxed and friendly, through to regional competitions that are more competitive but still with a friendly atmosphere, to national competitions that are taken very seriously. Of course, the further up the ladder you go, the harder races will be, but club meets bring a sense of team-spirit and belonging to a group of fellow athletes that is surprisingly rare for runners.

Summary

✓ *If your training hasn't been going well for several sessions at a time, then a change may be needed. Decide exactly what the problem is, and make simple adjustments to solve it—this could be done by introducing different types of sessions, shortening the length of your runs, or making your runs harder by upping the required speed.*

✓ *Entering races is a great way of putting what you've learned about yourself during training into practice. There are lots of opportunities for any runner to take part in an official event, and the popularity of these races will mean that you will always find someone at a similar level to race against.*

chapter 7

Warming Up, Cooling Down and Stretching

This chapter moves onto one of the most important, but also one of the most neglected, parts of a training session—performing a suitable and effective warm up. Particularly with those who run long distances (even runners who are relatively experienced), warm ups are often nothing more than a short run at a slower pace to that of the main running session. Now, this isn't a bad thing—in fact, jogging prior to a running session is recommended—however launching straight into a running session afterwards misses out something crucial to warming the body up sufficiently and preventing injuries or strains: dynamic stretching. Throughout this section, we will discuss recommended actions to perform during the warm up, and will give examples of useful stretches, drills and exercises that will go some way to helping us prevent ourselves from getting injured.

i Dynamic v Static Stretching

The first point is to clarify the differences between dynamic stretching—i.e. stretches performed while moving— and static stretching, in which the body holds stretches in a still position.

There are differences of opinion as to what should be done prior to a training session in terms of stretches, but modern science recommends performing dynamic stretches before you start running, with static stretches being left until the very end—during the cool down.

The reasoning for this decision is that dynamic stretches perform all the functions of 'warming' the body that static stretches don't. By moving while stretching, you will increase your heart rate and body temperature and put your body through the range of movement, and the movement patterns, it is going to perform during the main part of the training session. Opting for static stretching before a session would leave you cold, and your muscles wouldn't activate as they should. Although static stretching does stretch our muscles to the length that we need, it does not do so in the way that we use our muscles while running, so its usefulness before exercise is curtailed somewhat.

That isn't to say that static stretches are useless, though—they are ideal to use at the end of a session during the 'warm down', or 'cool down', as they help lengthen the muscles back to the state they were at before the session started.

ii How Important is Stretching?

In short: it is very, very important! There are five main reasons for stretching:

1. To improve flexibility.
2. To aid mobility for the session about to be undertaken.
3. To help prevent injuries.
4. To speed rehabilitation of the body after an injury.
5. To improve your recovery from a session.

Stretching should be performed before and after a training session. Before training we prepare the muscles for the activity and range of movement they are about to endure. Afterwards we can then restore the muscle length using static stretches.

Performing a 'stretching session' is also worthwhile as you return from injury and are restricted in the amount of training you can do, as this can help your body prepare itself for your return to running while expending very little energy. A good physiotherapist will be able to help you with the specifics of the muscles that are injured, both in terms of stretching and strengthening the area of concern.

Note that it is very important that you never force a stretch, whether dynamic or static. For every one that you do, you should go only to the point of tension—even if you're very inflexible and tension is felt very early into the stretch—and, if it's a static stretch, hold it there for the required time, whilst ensuring that your knees and feet are pointing in the same direction. Though decent flexibility is an important attribute for runners, we don't need to be as supple as a gymnast, as this actually makes creating the forces needed to generate power during exercise more difficult.

iii What Dynamic Stretches Should I Do?

Before a period of vigorous activity a gentle jog then stretches should be performed. The stretches should cover the whole of the body, including the arms and trunk, as the whole of the body will be moving while you're running—not just your legs!

Below are examples of some exercises you can do that would constitute an effective warm up for any running event. Overall, doing all of these dynamic stretches should take no longer than 10 minutes, so aiming to perform as many of these as possible before your run(s) will warm up your whole body—therefore helping all areas avoid injury—while not adding too much time onto your training (if your sessions are relatively time-constrained).

For each of these exercises, you should move into a position at which you can feel the muscles stretching, before moving onto the other body part/limb. They can be performed in any order, but we have arranged them below in the sequence most commonly used by those who train with Momentum Sports. Finally, though we have included pictures, you may find that you will want to watch videos of these stretches being performed, so that you can familiarise yourself with the exact technique. These stretches can be found at http://www.momentumsports.co.uk/TtDynamicStretches.asp

*Figure 7.1
Small Lunges*

Small Lunges

This is usually the first exercise that we do. To perform it, put your hands by your head and squeeze your shoulder blades together (not shown here)—this ensures that your back stays upright throughout the exercise and enhances the stretch— while bracing your stomach and back. Take small steps forward, dropping your back knee to about 6 inches above the ground (not touching it), and ensuring that your lower front leg remains vertical as you do the lunge.

High Knees

The aim of the High Knees exercise is to step quickly, bringing your knees to a fairly high level without having to lean backwards. Try and stay as light on your feet as you can during this exercise.

The High Knee exercise is often incorrectly used as a drill to try and improve technique—we want it to be gentle as to prevent overexertion, so short steps will be used throughout, and the level to which we bring our knees is higher than that of a 'natural' running style.

Heel Flicks

Similarly to the High Knees exercise, Heel Flicks will involve taking short steps—but this time you will flick your heels up to your backside, and there doesn't need to be any knee lift. Though many people perform this exercise with their hands behind their back, we would recommend that your arms mimic their action when running—any practice is good practice!

Hamstring Walks

For this simple but effective stretch, all you need to do is raise one straightened leg until you feel a stretch in your hamstring. It doesn't matter how high you can lift your leg, as the important thing is feeling the stretch, so don't kick wildly. Make sure that the heel of your other leg stays on the floor, as this also ensures that the stretch is a gentle one—it is important that we don't use too much force on our hamstrings during the warm-up.

*Figure 7.2
High Knees*

*Figure 7.3
Hamstring
Walks*

Figure 7.4
Calf Step-Backs
(Bent Leg)

Figure 7.5
Chest Stretch

Calf Step Backs

This exercise has two parts, which stretch different areas of the calf muscle in preparation for your running session. The common theme between the two parts is to step back into a calf stretch—i. e. keep a tall posture with one leg back, one leg forward, both feet facing forwards, and both heels in contact with the ground— first with a straight leg at the back, and then changing to a bent leg. Performing each part five times on each leg should be enough to stretch your calf muscles sufficiently.

Chest Stretch

The first of the upper body stretches is simple—start by raising your elbows to the sides until your upper arm is parallel with the floor, then swing your elbows back to 'open out' your chest. Perform this about 12 times.

Shoulder Stretch

This can be done straight after the chest stretch. Start by straightening your arms, and have one facing upwards with the other facing the ground. Then, reach as far back as you can with both arms, and then quickly swap so that the arm that was facing the sky is now facing the ground and vice versa. Keep alternating in this manner until you have done 16 stretches overall.

Sideways High Knees

Most of our movements while running are forwards, but there are cases where lateral movements are needed, such as running the bend of an athletics track or turning a corner during cross country/road races— this exercise just stretches off those lateral muscles.

This drill involves the same movement as the High Knees drill, but you will move sideways. Change direction by 180 degrees after about 10 metres.

Hamstring Lunges

This exercise involves the most 'intense' stretch, despite it not being very vigorous, so it would be best to leave this until the end. The first part of the exercise is a similar motion to the Small Lunge, but the lunge will be deeper (i.e. your front leg will land a bit further forward than in the Small Lunge). Then, pull back so that your front leg is straight and you feel a stretch in your hamstring.

After the dynamic stretches your body should be ready to take on more strenuous activity, and the stretches should help prevent any strains or pulled muscles from occurring. Ideally, the next part of your session will be to practice your running technique through some drills (see Chapter 8), but if you really are pushed for time then moving onto the main running session would be fine. Either way, dynamic stretches are neglected all too often by runners, and their usefulness cannot be emphasised enough. So, making sure that you perform these at least before going onto your main session will be much more beneficial to you than skipping dedicated warm ups completely.

Figure 7.6
Shoulder Stretch

iv What Should I do During the Cool Down?

The 'cool down', or 'warm down' is what takes place at the end of the session. During the main training session, your muscles will work hard and will produce waste products as a result, so cooling down properly is important. You should therefore aim to do an active cool down, involving jogging and stretches, after your main training session, as this will raise your heart rate slightly and pump more blood around the body—flushing these waste products away from the muscles.

We would recommend jogging or striding (at around 70% for 60-100m at a time) for five minutes, and then moving on to stretching key areas of the body. This part of the session is when static stretches are advisable—these return your muscles, which will have shortened slightly during the hard work of the main training session, to their original state at the beginning of the session. This will also reduce stiffness in the following days, and making sure that your muscles return to their original length can help with the prevention of injuries.

v Developmental Stretches

Lastly, we come to something that can be done away from the park or track: developmental stretches. These are usually performed as a session in their own right, and are very important for the long-term development of any runner.

Here we are basically referring to stretches that can be done specifically to improve your flexibility, through holding a stretch to the point of tension few a few seconds, waiting for the tension to ease off (without moving) and then increasing the stretch gradually and repeating the process (usually 3 repetitions in all). Performing these exercises several times a week will improve your mobility a lot – while not making yourself excessively flexible—and you will find that your increased suppleness will enable you to correct your technique more easily (see Chapter 8) and will lay the foundations to becoming stronger and faster.

Here we will give a few examples of developmental stretches for the most common 'problem' areas for runners:

Hip Flexor Stretch

While kneeling, place one foot forward—making sure that your front foot can be seen over the knee. Ease your hips forward and place your hands on your knees for balance. Increase the distance between your legs as the stretch progresses.

Hamstring Stretch

This stretch is fairly intensive, so err on the side of caution and don't worry if your hamstring flexibility is poor—just start from the first point at which you feel tension. Ideally, you will need a partner for this stretch. Lie on your back with both legs straight, and then lift one leg (still keeping it as straight as possible) until you feel a stretch in your hamstring. Once you feel a stretch, get your partner to apply gentle pressure to your leg, while you push your leg against their hands (if you're using a band, then pull your leg towards you while pushing against the band). After 10 seconds of this, relax, and then pull your leg (or get your partner to push it) towards you a little more, and repeat the same process.

Calf Stretch

This can be done either standing or with the aid of a wall/fence. Step back with one foot and bend your front knee, while ensuring that both your feet are facing forward. Your back heel should be on the floor at all times, and your back should be straight. To progress this stretch, increase the distance between your feet, still ensuring that your back heel doesn't leave the ground.

Glutes

Similarly to the Hamstring stretch, this exercise requires you to lie on your back. Raise your right leg and bend it so that the knee is at 90°. Keeping your shoulders and back as flat as possible to the floor, gently drop your knee towards the floor on your left— it will move over the other leg. Then, repeat for the other side. This exercise is difficult to progress, so 3 sets of the same 'difficulty' would be fine.

Quadriceps

This stretch targets the quads at the front of your upper leg, and is another one that is difficult to progress, so doing 3 sets of the same method is fine. While standing with a straight and upright back, bring one foot to your backside. Clasp that foot with one hand and ensure that your knees are kept together and that your standing leg is slightly bent, with the standing foot facing forwards. If you are struggling for balance, then you can use your free hand to steady yourself on a wall/chair (making sure that your back is still straight and knees are still together).

Summary

✓ *Dynamic stretching is recommended for your warm up rather than static stretching. By moving your muscles under controlled circumstances while stretching them, you can replicate the range of motion that they will go through during your actual session. This can't be achieved to the same extent by static stretching.*

✓ *Stretching is a very important part of running, as it increases your flexibility and aids your body's mobility, both of which will help safeguard against injury. Devoting some of your warm up to stretching the key areas of your body (hamstrings, calves, etc.) will be of enormous benefit in the long run.*

✓ *Stretching in between sessions is also beneficial, as increased mobility can be important in ensuring your running technique is efficient and effective— which will help you run quicker as time goes on.*

chapter 8

Running Technique

Here we come to the most important aspect of your running: your technique! No matter what level of runner you are, or whether you're a sprinter or an ultra-long distance athlete, the fundamentals of an efficient running technique are more or less the same—the only difference is the amount of effort required for each 'part'. Following the guidelines set out in this chapter will, in simple terms, enable you to run faster. You won't, however, want to change your running style so much that, as a result of wanting to keep to these principles, it becomes exaggerated and unnatural. Rather, you will want to gradually introduce yourself to the different aspects of the running style, and allow it to become second nature through regular practice and doing drills that specifically improve technique.

i The Fundamentals of Correct Running Technique

We normally consider there to be two parts to each running stride, which when optimised make for good running technique. These are the "**stance**" and "**flight**" phases—i.e. when we are in contact with the floor and when we are not, respectively. The only way we can derive power to propel ourselves forwards is when we are in contact with the ground (it is very hard to push or pull against the air!); this the stance phase. The flight phase is about recovering our legs so that we can generate that force efficiently when we do strike the ground.

Within these phases, there are five elements of our running action that need to be considered, and regular practice of each will allow you to perform them more naturally over time—resulting in a much smoother, more efficient and therefore faster running technique:

The five elements are **toe up**, **heel up**, **knee up**, **reach out** and **claw back**.

Toe Up, Heel Up and Knee Up

Toe up simply means generally keeping the angle of the foot to the shin at around 90 to 120 degrees and not pointing our toes (Figure 8.1). To achieve the heel up and knee up

Figure 8.1 (left) Keep the angle A to 90 - 120 degrees.

Figure 8.2 (right) Step over a point 6 inches above the floor.

43

phases, a good tip is to try and raise your leg to a certain height and use the opposite leg as guidance. Initially, we'd advise trying to step over a point on the stance leg (i.e. the one in contact with the ground) about 6 inches off the floor (Figure 8.2).

Reach Out

By this, we really just mean the forward motion of our leg. Clearly the further we reach, the longer our stride—but it has to be controlled as if we reach too far then we risk "putting the brakes on" (see 'Heel Striking' below). Figure 8.3 shows a good length for an endurance runner to reach out.

Claw Back

This is where we try to utilise one of Newton's laws of physics: throwing our bodies in the direction we wish to travel, by getting our foot moving backwards (i.e. 'clawing back') under our trunk to create an equal and opposite reaction. This is demonstrated by the left leg from Figure 8.3 through to Figure 8.4.

Figures 8.3 (left) and 8.4 (right)

As mentioned previously, all five of these 'elements' of the running action apply to all runners, though the amount of effort put into each will depend on the distance you're running—for example, a sprinter will need a much higher knee lift, enabling a much longer reach out and harder claw back, than a marathon runner.

ii Common Problems

We've had a look at what we *should* do as part of our running technique; now, we will examine some problems that could hamper your speed and increase your susceptibility to injury. The weaknesses that are listed are common errors for runners—and can be found even in those who have been training for a long time, particularly if they haven't had much guidance. Eliminating these problems early will put you in a very good position, ensuring that you progress in the correct way as you develop your running and experience.

Heel Striking

As the name suggests, this 'problem' will arise if you land with your heel first, which generally means it is too far in front of your body. This will act as a braking action to your running, as your foot will be striking in front of your centre of gravity. If you do this, a lot of work will then be needed to get your weight back over your heel—which goes against the above principle of 'clawing back' and fluently propelling yourself onto the next stride.

An additional danger is that heel striking increases the stress on your joints, as you will tend to land heavily if you do this.

We can think of running as being like riding a child's scooter. If we want to go faster, we paw at the ground with our forefoot very near the stance leg. If we wish to brake and slow down, we use our heel some way out in front of our bodies.

*Figure 8.5
An example of
heel striking.*

Leaning Backwards or Forwards

Ideally, we want our body to be leaning slightly forwards, though not bending at the waist. Leaning backwards again acts as a brake on each stride, and may put strain on your lower back.

This is again because the foot is likely to be hitting the ground some way in front of our centre of gravity.

If we lean too far forwards, it generally means that we aren't able to get adequate knee lift and as a result there isn't enough time within the stride to bring the foot contact far enough back.

Lateral Arms

The function of our arms when running is to bring balance to our bodies, countering the movement of our legs to avoid rotations that would lead to inefficient movements and potentially—particularly when fatigued—an inability to land our strides where we wish to.

The lateral arms problem occurs when your arms cross your body, as opposed to swinging through in the direction that you're travelling (see Figure 8.6 as an example). This means that you are not really using your arms for their purpose and you therefore will twist in a way which isn't desirable. Figure 8.7 is a better example of your arms' ideal position when swinging through.

Figures 8.6 (left) and 8.7 (right)

The height at the front and back of your arm swing will depend on the speed you are running. For sprinting (e.g. at the final stage of a race), your hands should come up to chin height at the front, and at the back your upper arm should come almost parallel with the ground at its furthest point. While running at slower paces, the range of movement will be decreased with an emphasis on balance and relaxation, but maintaining the principle of keeping your arms swinging in the direction of your run.

Finally, as a general rule of thumb, it is normally best not to let your elbow come in front of your hip.

Sitting as you run

This refers to your hips—if they're not held high enough, then you will give the impression that you are 'sitting' as you're running. This means you'll not be able to extend your stride as you should and will often contact the ground too far in front of your body as the lower hip carry means you don't have time to "claw back" (Figure 8.8). Generally speaking athletes who run like this end up using the muscles on the fronts of their legs, but don't utilise their hamstrings or calves very well.

'Pendulum Legs'

The issue that we've termed 'pendulum legs' is when your feet don't come far off the floor. This causes problems because you are pulling very long levers forwards as you pull your legs through—something which basic physics tells us is much harder work. As such the forward swing takes a

*Figure 8.8
An example of
'Sitting'.*

longer time than it should and we end up still moving the foot forwards as we hit the floor, causing a braking action. Figure 8.9 demonstrates the restrictions that having 'pendulum legs' can bring.

*Figure 8.9
'Pendulum Legs'.*

iii How Often Should I Work on my Technique?

Of course, if you want to run more efficiently then the first thing that would come to your mind is to practice it as quickly and as often as possible. This isn't really the best solution though, as it is almost impossible to work on all five 'fundamentals' of the running technique simultaneously, and the 'new' technique may be very different to your 'natural' one. Potentially this may cause a few strains if the range of movement is something that your body isn't familiar with.

To combat the problem of working on lots of different things at the same time, you can break down your technique into different parts—these are known as running drills. By concentrating on one or two aspects of your technique at a time, and practising each part several times before sessions, you can familiarise yourself with the feeling of the 'correct' execution of each phase much quicker. This in turn will help you bring all of it together into one efficient, fluid running action quicker than if you were to try and correct all parts of your technique immediately.

We would generally advise working on your technique only once or twice a week to start with, and these sessions should take the form of the running drills described below. Once you feel that you are starting to get the hang of the correct technique of each part, then you can try and implement the 'new' style into part of your training runs. Again, we wouldn't advise doing a whole five mile run with your adapted running style, as running in an unfamiliar way for a very long time could end up being counterproductive. However, you could decide to do 800m of a long run with an 'efficient' technique to start with—before reverting back to your 'natural' style—and then increase the amount of time/distance that you spend working on your improved technique gradually as the weeks go on.

iv What can I do to Work on my Technique?

Chapter 7 briefly mentioned performing running drills as part of your warm up, and that is the time we suggest would be best to work on them. If you find that you don't have time for drills while warming up, then make sure that you dedicate a session (perhaps during the weekend) to practising them—remember: the extra work will pay off if you can run more efficiently and therefore faster!

Though we have included pictures that hopefully will make the action of each drill clear, you may find that watching a video would be best. Videos of all the following drills can be found at: http://www.momentumsports.co.uk/TtDrillsEventSp.asp .

Step Over Drill

The aim of this drill is to do very small steps, in which you lift your foot over your ankle bone before lowering it to the floor, with the angle between your foot and your lower leg being decreased as much as possible—90 degrees is around the correct angle. In terms of the range of movement, this drill is similar to pedalling a bike—though our feet will only come up to the height of your lower shin.

One way to achieve this successfully is to have someone stand behind you, and to make sure that they can't see the soles of your shoes at all once you commence this drill.

The Step Over drill works on the Toe Up phase of the running action.

Single Leg Drill

As the name suggests, each time this drill is performed only one leg will be concentrated on. For this exercise, we are working on the Toe Up, Heel Up and Knee Up phases of our running technique.

The first part of the action is to create the small angle between your foot and leg as described in the Step Over Drill—this position will be maintained throughout. Then, pull your heel up to your backside. Once it is there, you will then bring your knee through to the front, to the highest position it will reach when you're running—this should be just below the level at which your upper leg is parallel to the ground.

The final part of this drill is to drop your foot to the ground and start again—take very small steps in between each action, and perform it on every third stride.

Straight Leg Drill

At first sight this may seem like a strange drill to help with our running, but it is very useful for the Toe Up and Claw Back phases of the running action—i. e. the beginning and the end of each stride.

The aim of this drill is to land on your forefoot, but with your legs straight (though not locked at the knees), and keeping your upper body straight—leaning forward slightly from the hips.

This drill is performed for two reasons: Firstly, it teaches you to pull your foot and toes up—if you don't, you'll stub your toes on the track; secondly, it teaches you to claw back at the end of each stride, by pulling your foot back and causing your foot to come in contact with the ground behind your centre of gravity—avoiding the braking action that would occur otherwise.

Heel Flick High Knees Drill with Run Off

This drill should come at the end of the drills section of your training session, as it puts all of the phases together. There are two parts to it—the 'high knee' part at the beginning will use the same action as the single leg drill, but this time it will be performed on every stride, and each stride will be fairly short. The second part—the 'run off' will involve extending your stride after around 30m into the full running action, while maintaining the 'toe up, heel up, knee up' principles as well as keeping your upper body upright.

Summary

✓ *There are two parts to each running stride—the stance and flight phases. These two phases are made of five components: toe up, heel up, knee up, reach out and claw back. The amount of effort put into each phase will differ depending on the speed you are running, but these principles apply to runners of all distances.*

✓ *There are a few weaknesses that are commonly found in beginners. Asking somebody to watch your technique— preferably an athletics coach—will help you identify any problems early on and thus make changes before poor technique becomes a habit.*

✓ *Introducing running drills into your warm up is a good way of breaking down 'textbook' running technique into manageable parts. Immediately incorporating all five components of an efficient running style into your own technique is very difficult, so working on one or two of them at a time through certain drills will enable you to familiarise yourself with each one individually. Then, once those drills become second nature, you can work on bringing them all together.*

Specialist Help

Although you may be able to create your own training plan and get on with training entirely by yourself, there will most likely come a time when specialist help is required. This usually comes about when injuries occur, as you may not know exactly what is wrong and will need someone more experienced to evaluate you problems, as well as give you specific advice to prevent recurrences. There are other areas that you may want help, however—perhaps you need confirmation that your running technique is correct, or you don't have time to construct a training plan and want somebody else to take that responsibility, in which case you may want to seek out a professional running coach. Here we will discuss the type of specialist help that you may come across or find beneficial during your running career.

chapter 9

i Coaches

If you are new to running, then chances are that the different phases and biomechanics of your running technique are completely new to you. Reading and brushing up on your knowledge of these aspects are of course useful, but you may not know how well you are implementing them without the help of somebody watching and giving advice. Although technically many people would be able to identify what you are and aren't doing, the extra knowledge and experience that a coach possesses can help you identify how to improve and *why* things are going wrong (if at all)—for example, giving you advice on exercises to perform to strengthen weak areas of your body.

Coaches can also be relied upon to set you a training schedule, which would take that responsibility away from you in case you don't have time to create a detailed plan, or you want some advice on what to do to improve it, or you simply want your training to be set by someone more experienced. Liaising with a coach, whether every week or less frequently, can also help you evaluate how much you are progressing from an independent standpoint, with advice on where to go next. This is important, as one of the key roles of a coach is to be objective in a way that it is very hard for an athlete to be about themselves, so the advice they give could be from a completely new perspective.

The last point to consider is whether the coach charges for sessions or for creating your training schedule. Many coaches don't charge anything for their services, but, while this means that money will be saved if you opt for them, it could also mean that the time they are able to spend discussing your progress and helping you with your training is limited. Full-time, paid coaches are able to spend their whole working life coaching, studying and learning, so more often than not would be more experienced and knowledgeable than those who only coach in their spare time. This is not always the case, but bear this in mind when thinking about whose help you should seek.

ii Masseurs

Massage is a very important area of sport nowadays, with a lot of advances in the fields of injury prevention and recovery. If you are training a lot and pushing yourself hard, then it may be worth seeking an appointment with a masseur to make your muscles more flexible, reduce the risk of injury and increase the potential workload that can be carried out by your muscles. All of these aspects could have a big impact on your ability to train and perform at your highest level. Generally, the more frequently you train during the week, the more often you should have a massage, as there will potentially be more tightness, knots (sections of muscle that constrict and cause pain) and adhesions (a type of scar tissue) in your muscles.

A more detailed analysis of the benefits of sports massage can be found in Chapter 17, Part iii.

iii Physiotherapists

For the purpose of this section, 'physiotherapy' will refer to the process of diagnosing injuries, the causes of injuries, and suggesting exercises and stretches to help treat the problem. Sometimes this can be done by masseurs (mostly for more minor problems), but it is usually better to seek out a professional who specialises in anatomy, physiology and/or biomechanics to identify weak areas that are at risk of developing into injuries in the future. They will also be able to find underlying causes of recurring or chronic problems (e. g. to do with lifestyle, muscular imbalances, etc.), and to suggest ways of improving weak areas of the body.

Physiotherapists will use a range of techniques and exercises to help diagnose the root of the problems that you are encountering, and may set rehabilitation programmes for you to follow to aid your recovery and strengthen the problematic areas to, hopefully, prevent recurrence of injuries in the future. They should also be the first port of call for recovery from more serious musculoskeletal conditions and bone breakages, as they will be able to guide you through exercises to help you restore movement and normal body functions.

iv Nutritionists/Dieticians

Nutritionist or dietician? We are simply talking about someone who can advise you on what and when to eat! Technically, dieticians are the ones you will want to search for as that is the legally-protected term (they are state registered and follow a regulated code of practice—visit www.bda.uk.com). Anyone can claim to be a nutritionist without necessarily having qualifications, so we advise you inquire about any professional's background before going through with a consultation. Though information on healthy diets, sporting diets and healthy/unhealthy foods can be found in countless books, articles and websites, you will only find more general information in these sources. A dietician will be able to look at your own diet and advise you on what changes to make in order to cut your body fat or improve protein/carbohydrate/vitamin intake where necessary, which can be a vital component in you maximising your running potential. They may also be able to give you a professional measurement of your body fat, which is another factor that can be useful in helping you decide what changes (if any) need to be made to your diet.

v Drawbacks of Outside Help

The benefits of each specialist area that we listed above are the 'best case scenario', so to speak. As with most things in life though, you should be a little wary and know exactly what experience, advice or services you're looking for before you commit to enlisting somebody for help. Of course, anybody that gives you advice will be doing so in the best faith possible, but bear in mind that it may not be applicable or suitable for runners, and that some experts are far better than others.

This is the first point to consider—is the person that you are seeing experienced with dealing with runners? This applies in particular to nutritionists and masseurs—the requirements of runners (calorie requirements in nutrition, deep tissue work in massage) differ from the requirements of those that don't exercise frequently, or even those that do other sports, so there is a danger that advice or treatment will give you little benefit for the practicalities of running. Likewise, you should also make sure that any coaches you see are experienced in your area of running, as those who only coach sprinters may not know what advice to give long-distance runners, and vice versa. One way to ensure that the advice you'll be getting is correct and practical for your sport is to check what qualifications and experience the expert has, and if they are specific to running requirements. There are also dedicated websites that list masseurs, nutritionists, physiotherapists, etc. who are fully qualified to treat sportsmen and women. As a general rule of thumb, don't go for 'experts' who have attended only weekend-long courses during their time in the trade.

The other main drawback of seeking specialist help is the cost. Inevitably, you will have to pay for the services of masseurs, physios, coaches and nutritionists, so you will need to be absolutely sure that you want or need assistance before committing yourself to an appointment. Like a lot of services, too, you generally get what you pay for, so experts that charge higher rates will tend to be more experienced and thus more likely to help you quicker than those that are cheaper. This isn't always the case, however—remember to check their qualifications and *with whom* their experience was built before anything else. Generally, we would suggest that all of these areas of specialisation are worth exploring, but make sure that you know the costs and have explored the cheaper alternatives (searching online for training tips/asking friends or teammates for dietary advice, etc.) before following through with your meeting with a specialist.

Summary

✓ *A running coach can help you with your training schedule if you need assistance. They can also adopt a more informal role for you, and simply give their feedback on your technique, your strengths and weaknesses, and the sort of sessions you are doing.*

✓ *Receiving sports massages is a very important and oft-neglected part of a runner's career. Seeing a masseur every so often will help your muscles recover from the rigours of training and decrease the likelihood of injuries.*

✓ *Physiotherapists are the people to go to if you obtain an injury that severely restricts your ability to run. They will be able to diagnose the problem and, more importantly, give you advice on exercises, stretches, etc. to do to help with your recuperation.*

✓ *Nutritionists will be able to give you useful information on the suitability of your diet and the amount of body fat that you have, which you can then use to make adjustments and ensure that your diet isn't undoing all of the hard work you put in during training.*

✓ *Before seeking help from an outside source, try to determine how much experience the professional has had with sportspeople. In certain areas of lifestyle, runners require different things to those who live relatively sedentary lives, so some information that you are given may not be entirely suitable.*

chapter 10

Recovery

The distances that you run, the times that you achieve, and the amount of times that you train a week will all be important factors in your progression from a beginner athlete to a more experienced, stronger, fitter one. There is one other aspect to your training, though, that is often overlooked by runners despite being just as important, if not more so, than anything else: recovery. Though it would make sense that running for longer will result in you becoming fitter and stronger, having enough rest in between sessions is just as important as the exercise that you actually undertake; have too little rest, and you will find that running at your optimum level is impossible. Here we discuss how much recovery you should give yourself during and after training—depending on your strength and experience, what can be done during 'recovery' days, and the purpose that recovery serves.

i The Importance of Recovery

Think about when you feel strongest during a training session—would you say you feel fittest at the beginning of a session, during a run, or after you've completed your training? If we define fitness or 'strength' to be the ability to perform at your best, then clearly we would say that this is at the start of training, before any strenuous exercise has taken place. Once you have started running, or have completed a couple of runs, then tiredness begins to set in, and your ability to run your fastest starts to wane. This feeling will be exacerbated even more after a hard training session—often after an intensive run, you will feel unable to run a few metres, let alone a few miles, so this in itself proves that you are stronger at the beginning than at the end of a training session!

If your body hasn't had time to recover from previous training sessions, then you will be—starting subsequent sessions from a position of being less fit than the last time you trained – in other words, you may start a session on Tuesday at 90% fitness, having begun training on Monday at 100%. Though there will inevitably be occasions like this during a training program, if you make a habit of it then you will find yourself becoming less fit and needing an increasingly longer amount of time to get back up to speed. You will also find that being tired at the beginning of a session will mean an increased likelihood of failing to make your times or having to drop out completely, which will somewhat limit the usefulness of training and could lead to slower times in the future.

The graph below displays how a lack of sufficient recovery can affect an athlete in comparison to one athlete that allows their body to recuperate and does fewer but higher quality sessions during the week:

Fitness Over Time for two Athletes of Differing Training Regimes

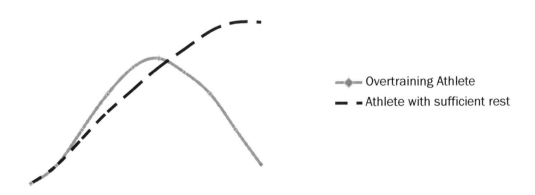

— Overtraining Athlete

- - Athlete with sufficient rest

Note that an overtraining athlete will probably see more of an improvement during the first few sessions than their resting counterpart, but this advantage will quickly be lost and even reversed if the excessive amount of training is kept up.

Simply speaking, at the end of a session your body prepares to repair itself and build up for the next time you start running again, in order to cope with the pressures better. To receive the full benefits of this very useful capability, you will need to give your body enough time to fully repair itself.

ii How Much Recovery Should I Have?

During your Training

The first part of your recovery that you should think about is during your session—this can apply both to sessions in which several runs will be undertaken, and also to long, steady runs. Knowing how much recovery to give yourself in order to find the session challenging but doable is difficult.

Of course, trial and error will play a part in deciding how much recovery should be taken for interval sessions, but a good guide for beginners is to take your heart rate after the first run, and then time how long it takes for your pulse to return below 100 beats per minute (unless you walked the entire distance of your run, your pulse should be well above 100!). This time can then be used as a basis for setting the recovery during future sessions, and it can even be used as a handy short-term goal. For example, lowering the time it takes for your pulse to return to 100 by 30 seconds over the course of the first month.

You can also help with your ability to carry on a long, steady run by taking on water or carbohydrates (for example, an energy bar or isotonic drink) while you are running. Doing this will give you an extra energy boost to keep your pace up for longer and quickly replace the fluids you will have lost in the early part of your run.

As has been emphasised earlier on in this book, erring on the side of caution is highly recommended in the first weeks of your training. At no point should you feel absolutely drained or faint at the end of a run or at the end of a session—if you do, then immediately set the next day (at least) as a recovery day and plan to take it much easier the next time around.

After your Training

The amount of recovery that you have after a training session is another aspect that will need to be played around with before you discover what is right for you, but for the first few weeks we would advise taking a rest day after each session you do, in order to allow your body to recover from the unfamiliar rigour of running. After that, you may start to think about training on consecutive days, but limit this to only once instance per week (i. e. you may train on Monday and Tuesday, but make sure that Wednesday is completely free). The final stage would be to train on consecutive days a couple of times a week, but we would recommend leaving this until you have three months of training under your belt.

iii What Should I do on Recovery Days?

Obviously, resting is the most recommended answer to the above question. If you have a busy week training-wise, with four to five hard days a week, then completely abstaining from vigorous exercise on your recovery days would be the best way to allow your body to recover sufficiently. For those who do fewer running sessions in a week, however, you may wish to do some gentle exercise in the form of cycling, swimming, walking etc. to keep yourself active while not tiring yourself out so much as to be exhausted when your next training session does come along. Stretching is also a good idea on recovery days as this too will assist recovery and maintain running range of movement, while keeping rested.

When an important race comes along, then you will want to leave a few days (maybe two to three) before the event as recovery days. During these occasions, it may be worth performing a gentle warm-up to keep yourself supple and ensure that your muscles are free of as many waste products as possible before your competition comes along. Otherwise, resting completely (apart from essential everyday tasks of course!) is the best course of action to take to ensure that you're prepared for the big day. Make sure that you eat and drink well, too, so that you have as much of the correct fuel as possible for the competition.

In the end, everyone will find a solution that works for them, and experimenting with complete rest and gentle exercise every now and again to stave off boredom will ensure that you find your favourite routine—enabling you to be as ready as you can for each training session and competitive race.

Summary

✓ *Having enough recovery is one of the most important aspects of your training. Without allowing your body to recover, you will eventually find that training becomes much harder and consequently has less value.*

✓ *Experiment with the recovery that you give yourself both in between repetitions during a training session, and in between sessions. If you start a training session feeling very lethargic, you may need to give yourself more time to recuperate.*

✓ *Recovery days don't have to be completely devoid of activity. Stretching or activities that are gentler on your legs, such as swimming, are good ways of keeping yourself active and in good shape without tiring yourself out.*

Chapter 11

Nutrition and Supplements

Sports nutrition is a very broad and very complex subject, and this chapter will only explore a small amount of the available material and options for runners. Throughout this chapter we will give advice that is practical for runners and, while not written by a professional sports nutritionist, has been gathered by spending years studying and listening to experts - for an individual assessment of requirements, however, we would advise that you seek opinions from professionals in the subject. It should also be noted that following this advice won't necessarily bring you good results if your lifestyle does not compliment your nutrition intake (more detailed information on this can be found in Chapter 12).

¡ What Should I Eat?

Broadly speaking, as runners we are looking to eat the correct amount of protein, carbohydrates and fats, as well as vitamins and minerals, to help us have enough fuel and nutrients to get us through training and competitions and develop our bodies to make ourselves faster, stronger and fitter. Runners differ from your everyday, sedentary person in that their active lifestyle requires more calories and a more delicate balance of nutrients than simply eating enough to stop being hungry.

How we get our protein, carbohydrates and fats is up to the individual. There are no 'rules', per se, but there are foods that are generally seen as useful for athletes and those that are to be avoided as much as possible. As long as your diet is balanced and healthy though, then there is no reason to not treat yourself to a sugary snack or indulge in some chocolate once in a while!

Protein

Our bodies are built with proteins. To build more muscle, repair muscles that have been used in training, and to repair injuries, we need a good supply of proteins from our diet. Generally, those of us who regularly eat meat will have a stable supply of protein in our diet already, but we need to make sure that we have a suitable amount—too little and we won't recover quickly after sessions, and if we have too much then the excess will just get stored as fat in our body.

For a scientific measurement of our ideal protein intake, we can use information on the levels of activity we do, the type of activity, and how much we weigh. The following is a fairly accurate guideline using to your body weight:

Endurance Athletes: 1.2 – 1.4g per kg

Power Athletes: 1.6 – 1.8g per kg

So, if you are an endurance athlete who weighs 60kg, then 80g of protein per day would be your ideal intake. If you are a power athlete who weighs 80kg, then this intake increases to 140g per day. This may well be covered by your normal diet anyway, but it is worth recording what you eat for a few days so you can make adjustments if necessary. Furthermore, vegans and vegetarians in particular should monitor their protein intake as the absence of meat means that it will be lower than that of meat eaters.

So, what foods contain good quantities of protein? The most common sources of protein (which contains four calories per gram) are:

Fish	Nuts	Lean Meat	Eggs
Poultry	Beans	Cheese	

These should all be bought fresh for the biggest benefit—although processed meats and ready meals will contain some protein, the high salt and high fat content makes them less healthy options.

Carbohydrates

These are to humans what petrol is to your car—without carbohydrates, we don't run properly! There are two types of carbohydrates—simple and complex. Simple carbohydrates are basically sugars such as glucose, while complex carbohydrates are mostly made up of starches.

You may have heard of the Glycaemic Index, or GI, which has been devised to give us information on how sugary foods are. It is useful to find out the GI of foods you eat, as the higher the index, the greater the fluctuations in the blood's glucose and insulin levels—this can lead to a condition called hypoglycaemia, in which our blood sugar is very low and we feel lethargic. In order to avoid this, you should not eat more than 150 calories of highly sugary foods in the hour before training.

Complex carbohydrates are the preferred option in a diet because they are better at storing vitamins, minerals and fibre. However, this is not to say that simple carbohydrates are useless and should be avoided at all costs—during and immediately after training, your body will be craving sugar to keep going or to start the recovery process. You should then have a meal containing complex carbohydrates within two hours of finishing training (the sooner the better, if you can stomach it). Simple carbohydrates can also help give you an energy boost immediately before you set out to do a session—around 100 calories of highly sugary foods up to an hour before training may help you feel more energised and alert.

One more note is that wholemeal versions of carbohydrate-rich foods are recommended as they contain much higher levels of fibre, which take longer to absorb and therefore gives you energy for longer, than their refined, 'white' alternatives (bread and pasta being the main two examples.

Below is a list of foods rich in carbohydrates (which contain four calories per gram), split into the simple and complex varieties:

Simple Carbs

Sugar	Sweet	Chocolate
Honey	Sweet Cereals	Fruits—particularly dried and ripe ones

Complex Carbs

Bread	Most types of rice	Pasta
Potatoes	Unprocessed Beans	Skimmed Milk

Remember: simple carbohydrates are best eaten during or an hour either side of training, whereas complex carbohydrates should be consumed regularly as part of your diet.

Sticking to this simple principle should allow you to feel energised while you run, while allowing you to maintain a healthy diet and with it your weight.

Fats

Fats are essential for healthy living—it helps form the structure of our body tissues, helps with hormone metabolism within the body, and cushions our organs and body parts. However, the majority of the population consume too much fat, or at least the saturated, unhealthy kind, and thus have too much fat to be able to run to their potential.

In short, the suggested amount of fat in your diet is 25% of your total calorific intake. There are 9 calories in every gram of fat, so use this as a guideline when deciding what food to include in your diet. These should be primarily unsaturated fats, as these are much healthier than the saturated kind—generally, it is advised that men avoid having more than 30g of saturated fat a day, with that figure 20g for women.

So, what foods contain each type of fat?

Saturated Fats

Fatty cuts of meat	**Cheese**	**Chocolate confectionery**
Butter and lard	**Cakes and Pastries**	**Cream, sour cream and ice cream**

Unsaturated Fats

Lean meats	**Nuts and seeds**
Oily Fish—salmon, mackerel, haddock	**Sunflower oil, olive oil**
Some fruit and vegetables, e. g. avocado	

Vitamins and Minerals

These can be thought of as catalysts for the body— certain amounts are needed to make it function properly, but you won't be able to make it run 'better' by overloading on these micronutrients; once these are doing their jobs, no matter how much you have, they can't do any more for you.

Some vitamins and minerals are more key for runners than others. The following are the most important for athletes:

Vitamin/Mineral	What does it do?	Found in:
Vitamin B	Helps release energy from food and makes nerves and muscle tissues	Eggs, bread, fish, rice

	function properly	
Vitamin C	Well-known for protecting against colds, this is also useful for hard structures in the body, such as teeth, bones and cartilage.	Oranges, red/green peppers, Brussels sprouts, potatoes
Vitamin E	Helps with maintenance of the immune system.	Plant oils, nuts, seeds
Omega 3	Helps counter heart disease	Oily fish – salmon, tuna, sardines
Calcium	Vital for strengthening bones, and ensuring blood clots normally	Milk, cheese, broccoli, cabbage, soya beans
Iron	Helps make red blood cells	Meat, beans, dried fruit, wholegrains
Magnesium	Assists in turning food we eat into energy	Wholegrain bread, fish, meat, dairy foods
Potassium	Controls balance of fluids in the body	Bananas, vegetables, fish, chicken
Zinc	Helps make new cells and enzymes, aids healing of wounds	Shellfish, milk, bread, cheese
Folic Acid	Forms healthy red blood cells	Broccoli, spinach, peas

ii When Should I Eat?

Broadly speaking, this will vary from runner to runner, and some experimentation may be needed, but most the 'rules' below will apply and make sense to most athletes.

Pre-exercise

This area will particularly require experimentation, in order to ensure that you don't feel lacking in energy while running, but equally that you won't experience stomach cramps from taking too much food and drink on board.

First of all, the time that you eat pre-exercise is dependent on the time of day that you will be running. If you will be running early in the morning, then you may not be able to eat much before you run. If you do have time to put something together, then a medium-sized breakfast that is low in fat, such as a large bowl of cereal, would be the best thing to consume. Otherwise, a smaller meal, or a drink with carbohydrates at least (such as a sports drink or a smoothie) can be taken on board if you don't have time to make anything larger.

If you are running in the early-to-mid afternoon, then a snack of 200-400 calories around two hours before you run (in addition to other your meals—make sure that you still eat breakfast and lunch!) would be the recommended course of action. Make sure that this snack isn't full of sugar, in order to avoid big changes in your body sugar levels.

This advice would also apply if you leave your training session until the evening. Generally, the largest meal of the day is eaten in the evening, but you may find that switching your biggest meal to lunchtime will be better for you in the long run.

Post-exercise

Your body will be depleted after a run, so it is important to refuel as soon as possible. A good idea is to have a banana or other fruit, a fruit smoothie, some sweets or low-fat biscuits as soon after training as you can. You should then try to eat a main meal with plenty of complex carbohydrates (e. g. potatoes, rice or pasta) and protein (e.g. meat/nuts) within a couple of hours—this will allow your body to gain enough fuel to rebuild muscle tissue, which naturally becomes damaged after prolonged exercise.

Throughout the Day

It is recommended that runners eat little and often throughout the day—this avoids taking on too many calories in one go for your body to handle—with the size of your large meals reduced (particularly the evening meal). It is also worth keeping a drink with you throughout the day, as you will generally need a total of 2-3 litres of water to perform at your best.

Races

The topic of nutrition on race day is discussed in Chapter 15, Part iv., alongside all other preparation that you will want to do on the day of an event.

iii I Want to Lose Weight—What Should I do?

The biggest danger for those who want to lose weight is not eating enough. As what we consume fuels us, one might think it makes sense that simply eating very little and exercising more often is the way to lose the pounds. This can have an adverse effect on your energy levels and even your health, however, so it is not at all advisable. The best course of action is to make sensible, slight alterations in diet—i. e. eating the same amount of food, but replacing any fatty foods with ones that have a higher carbohydrate content, while increasing the amount of exercise you undertake. This is a much more sustainable, and ultimately healthier, way of losing weight without making radical lifestyle changes. Generally, the best way to know that you are balancing weight loss with a healthy lifestyle is to lose no more than 1kg per fortnight (or 1lb per week).

As far as effort required to lose weight—each mile that you do typically burns 120 calories. Interestingly, it doesn't really matter how fast you do this, as it is primarily the distance covered that matters in terms of weight loss.

iv What Supplements are Useful?

If you have a healthy, balanced diet, then chances are that you are okay with what you're eating and don't need much in the way of supplementation to your diet, if at all. We would say that, at beginner's level, the benefits of supplements with large amounts of protein, creatine, oats, etc. are so insignificant as to be a waste of money—there is still a debate on the usefulness of these supplements for elite athletes, in fact. As such, we would recommend that you avoid going down the potentially expensive route of weight loss tablets, strength supplements, etc.

Vitamin Insurance

One option that we would say may be recommended is, however, taking a multivitamin tablet once a day, to ensure that you get a consistently good level of vitamins and minerals. This should simply be a back-up to a good diet, and should not replace it—the aim is to insure yourself against missing out on vital vitamins and minerals as a result of a gap in your normal diet.

If you have a healthy diet then this may not even be necessary, but if you do feel that you need to invest in multivitamin tablets, go for own-brand labels as these tend to be significantly cheaper than 'specialised' brands.

Summary

✓ *Take some time to read through the guidelines expressed in each section above. There is no need to adopt the latest 'fad' diet. Simply making sure that you give yourself the correct amount of protein, carbohydrates and fats each day will go a long way to ensuring that your nutritional intake is complimenting the work you're doing in training.*

✓ *Eating little and often throughout the day is generally thought to be the most ideal habit for runners to prevent the feeling of being bloated. Make sure to have a meal before you take part in an event during the day—two hours before is the best time for a main meal, with carbohydrates and fluids to keep yourself 'topped up' in the meantime. If you train in the evening, change your main meal of the day from dinner to lunch. This will prevent discomfort during the training session from having taken on too much food and not allowed it to digest properly.*

✓ *Supplements are not vital, and protein bars certainly aren't for beginners to running. Vitamin tablets are probably the most beneficial, but even these aren't necessary if you already eat a lot of fruit and vegetables and have a balanced diverse diet.*

Chapter 12

Lifestyle

As Chapter 11 discussed, your progress in training and competitions isn't just dependent on the amount of effort you put in on the track or on the road— your lifestyle away from training and the 'active' side of your daily routine can be just as important, if not more so. Whereas the previous chapter looked at the dietary requirements and recommendations to compliment your training as much as possible, this one looks to explore the activities that you get up to when you're not doing repetitions or long runs. Having a hectic schedule can make you very tired and have an adverse effect on your energy levels during exercise, which in turn will affect your progress in training and potentially undo all of the hard work you've put in. You therefore may need to manage your time more effectively, in order to allow yourself to hit your training sessions as hard as possible and reap the benefits.

i What Sort of Changes Will I Need to Make?

This will all depend on your job, social activities away from running, family commitments, etc. so a definitive answer would be impossible to give. However, keeping to the following guidelines should give yourself a balanced and healthy enough lifestyle to improve your chances of achieving your goals:

Smoking

This is an obvious problem for runners as it damages the lungs, which are vital for maintaining the flow of oxygen to your body. If you are a smoker, then quitting will put you in a much better position!

Alcohol

Drinking alcohol won't necessarily damage your health or chances of feeling energised for training—as long as it's in moderation. Bear in mind that alcohol dehydrates the body (though this can be countered somewhat by drinking water in between alcoholic beverages) and contains a lot of 'empty' calories that won't be of any use to runners—so it may undermine any efforts to lose weight. Alcohol also inhibits muscle protein synthesis, which is needed to rebuild muscles during your recovery between sessions, so drinking immediately after training especially isn't recommended. By no means do we recommend abstaining completely, but we would advise thinking carefully about how and when you drink alcohol.

Sleep

Because of the nature of what we do, runners need more sleep than most people. Poor sleep (e. g. under 6 hours a night) is usually the result of runners trying to cram all of their training into their lives, while not missing out on social gatherings. A lack of sleep does lead to deterioration of all aspects of a person's life, but performance levels in exercise will be a direct threat to your training and ability to progress. This can manifest itself in both physical and mental sluggishness, which will affect cardiovascular performance and a tendency to lose motivation. In summary—sleep is important!

Diet

Though Chapter 11 discusses this in more detail, it is always worth emphasising how much of a role your nutrition can play in determining whether you will succeed in reaching your goals or not.

Body Fat

The amount of fat that you carry can be affected by the above aspects of your lifestyle. It may be worth buying a kit to measure your own body fat percentage, or you can get a more accurate guide from a nutritionist/fitness professional.

Ideal, 'healthy' levels of body fat varies depending on your gender and your age. The following tables are a good guide:

Women

Age	Unhealthily Low	Healthy	Overweight	Obese
20-40 years	Under 21%	21-33%	33-39%	Over 39%
41-60 years	Under 23%	23-35%	35-40%	Over 40%
61-79 years	Under 24%	24-36%	36-42%	Over 42%

Men

Age	Unhealthily Low	Healthy	Overweight	Obese
20-40 years	Under 8%	8-19%	19-25%	Over 25%
41-60 years	Under 11%	11-22%	22-27%	Over 27%
61-79 years	Under 13%	13-25%	25-30%	Over 30%

Source: Gallagher et al, 2000:694-701

Elite athletes are at the lowest end of the healthy range of body fat. If you are towards the higher end of the healthy column, or have ventured into 'overweight', it may be worth looking to trim down your body fat, as this will simply be extra weight that you are carrying around. If you try running with a 10kg backpack, you'll see how much you're restricting yourself by being heavier than you need to be!

ii Work and Other Commitments

Work is often a big hurdle that athletes have to overcome in order to train as often as they want to, and to keep motivated and alert while training—with varying levels of success. Though sometimes a hectic work schedule is unavoidable, and sometimes work must take priority over leisure, we would recommend spending as much of your free time as possible keeping active, as running promotes a healthy physical and mental wellbeing that very few workplaces can.

The key to fitting in your running around work and other commitments is time management and planning each week. As you might have done while preparing for exams in school, it may be worth creating a timetable, with each day divided into distinct periods of what you hope to achieve.

Summary

✓ *There is a wide range of factors that will determine how ideal your lifestyle is and how conducive it is to running at your full potential. Smoking, excess alcohol consumption, a poor diet and a lack of sleep are all things that will have a negative impact on your ability to perform at your best, so a change (or in some cases, better management) will be needed if any of these apply to you.*

✓ *Finding out your percentage of body fat will be a useful guide as to how far off your 'ideal' shape you are. Don't worry if you're classed in an unflattering category—there is plenty of time to change!*

chapter 13

Psychology

A part of a runner's life that perhaps doesn't get as much attention as others is psychology—namely, how a runner prepares themselves mentally for races, how they cope with the lows that will inevitably occur at some point during the year, how they motivate themselves to push that much harder in training to achieve their goal, and many other alternatives. This chapter will explore the area of sports psychology and give you advice on various areas of mental preparation for races, keeping yourself motivated for training throughout the season, etc. Though not that of a professional sports psychologist, the advice given in this section has been accrued over many decades of experience, from extreme lows to amazing highs, and is constructed in a general, practical guide for all runners.

i How can I Cope with Nerves/Stress Before a Race?

This will tend to be the situation in which runners become most nervous, or most want to get 'fired up' about. Though being nervous isn't necessarily a bad feeling to have before an important race, feelings of stress, demotivation or extreme tension are things that you will want to avoid—they can have a severely negative influence on your performance. Managing stress levels is therefore a key skill that runners should learn, and this can be brought about in several different ways.

Progressive Muscular Relaxation

With practice, this technique can help you relax before a major competition or a race that you are worried about. It requires lying on the floor and progressively tensing and relaxing certain muscle groups. It would be best to spend 10 minutes or so on this when you first perform it, and in the comfort of your own home.

Whilst taking slow controlled deep breaths, start with the arms—make a fist and tighten all of the arm muscles (try to focus on relaxing all other muscles while doing this), and keep this tension for 5-7 seconds before relaxing for 30 seconds. Then, do the same for the neck, face, shoulders, upper back, lower back, hips and legs (in that order) and finish it all off by tensing all of your muscles and relaxing fully.

Mental Imagery / Visualisation

A good way of coping with your feelings (positive or negative) before a race is to imagine a variety of possible scenarios in your head in the days/hours leading up to the competition. A lot of the counterproductive feelings of stress and anxiety before a race stem from the 'unknown', so if your mind has already experienced and positively managed the stressful scenario in the comfort of your home, then it is more likely that you will be able to manage the scenario when it happens for real.

Furthermore, there are theories that suggest that imagining a sporting technique will cause the nervous system and muscles to react in a very similar way to actually performing the action for real, so mental imagery would further improve your muscle memory of sporting techniques.

As you become more adept at mental imagery, then you should start to imagine that all of your feelings leading up to the race are positive, whether they are normally associated with positivity or not. For example, a statement such as "just before a race, my heart is pounding and I feel very nervous" could be changed to "my heart is pounding, which means oxygen is getting around my body for the race, and my nerves are a sign that I'm ready for the challenge".

Practising this technique before a training session, especially if the training session is particularly tough or similar to an upcoming race, will help you perfect the technique of mental imagery and will hopefully allow you to channel any stress or anxiety before a race into something positive. Coupling mental imagery with the muscular relaxation technique described above is also a very good combination.

Positive Talk

As touched upon in the 'Mental Imagery' segment, something as simple as a positive mental attitude can help you calm your nerves before a race. For example, a negative thought before a half-marathon may be "this race will be hard and painful", but changing that attitude to one of "after this race, I will be more experienced in half-marathons and they will get easier from now on" can be beneficial.

Likewise, thinking of races as learning experiences regardless of the outcome could help you ease your anxiety—if the race doesn't go well, so what? There will be plenty of opportunities to have another go, and when the next competition comes along, you will have a better idea of what you would do differently to achieve a better result.

ii What can I do to Keep Motivated?

There may be times that you struggle to keep up your motivation to carry on training and working hard to improve. It may be a case of an injury lay-off undoing your hard work, a race that didn't go well, boredom due to an overly familiar routine, or other factors. In this section, we will give you some advice on how to keep yourself motivated to train and keep up your running at the best level you can.

Training Partners

Training alone can be a lonely, unfulfilling endeavour. Though some runners enjoy being able to chill out, be in their own bubble, and listen to some motivating music while going out for a session, there will be times that they yearn for a chat with a friend or fellow runner during training. Not only can a training partner be a solution to this, but they can also push you to a degree that is almost impossible while running by yourself. Although you can of course run quickly alone, sometimes you won't realise how fast you can potentially run unless you chase someone else down. Being able to compare your times with someone else close to you can be a big incentive to push on in training and make sure you beat your friends!

Joining a Club

Chapter 18 discusses this is more depth, but joining a club can be an inspiring course of action for a runner to take. Through this method, training partners can easily be found, and feeling as though you are part of a team chasing a collective goal in club competitions can be motivating. Chances are that the friends you make at a running club will enter plenty of individual competitions throughout the year, and entering an event with a group that you are familiar with can help with the nerves that come with racing. Furthermore, bringing a bit of competition between club mates, and the banter that comes with it, into your running can bring about a new lease of life!

Goal Setting

As described in more detail in Chapter 3, Part iii, setting yourself goals is a good way of keeping yourself motivated to continue with your running. Just remember that goals that you set yourself should be specific, able to be measured and monitored, realistic, and they should have a specific 'end' date on which you can look back on what you've achieved and evaluate if you succeeded. They can even be as simple as entering or completing a particular race. Remember, also, that you can set yourself a mixture of short term and long term goals to keep yourself working on the overall aim, thus not allowing yourself to get bored or give up. Having a target to aim at is an important component of training for elite and amateur athletes alike, and gives the hard work that you put in an explicit purpose.

Summary

✓ *Nervousness before a big event isn't necessarily something that will hinder how well the competition goes. If that feeling becomes one of stress or irritation though, then it may be worth experimenting with the various relaxation techniques.*

✓ *Sometimes, you may struggle to become motivated to do a particular session or to keep up your training as a whole. Making new friends who can become training partners, joining an official athletics/runners' club, or setting yourself new goals can all help stave off boredom or bring a renewed enthusiasm for the sport.*

Chapter 14

Race Day

So, you've been making your target times or distances in training, you feel fit and raring to go, and you want to test yourself against several opponents. The best way to do this, of course, is to enter a race. Everybody reacts differently to race day—some will become incredibly nervous and edgy, while others will stay relaxed and buoyant. In the end, you will discover your own ideal preparations and 'rituals' for competitions that will stand you in the best stead possible, but here we will give you a few tips on how to prepare for race day when you're still taking your first, tentative steps.

i What can I Expect on Race Day?

If you have never raced before, then the unknown nature of what you're getting yourself in for may add to the anxiety and nerves that you feel before the competition. Depending on where you're racing and what type of race you are taking part in, there will be slightly different facilities available to runners, and different regulations such as where you can warm up, where you need to go to register for the race, what you will need to bring with you, etc. Generally, no matter what competition you're going in for, we would suggest arriving at the venue no later than an hour before your race. Some events require an even earlier attendance, so make sure to check what the rules for your competition are.

Park Runs

Entering Park Runs is usually free, but requires prior registration. Since there is no real 'arena' to go to like there is during track meets, you will need to make sure that you know the location of the starting area and, depending on how you're travelling, its nearest entrance, car park or station. Once you arrive at the starting area, you will need to sign in using your proof of registration (this could be an email, a code, a barcode in some regions, etc.) and you will receive your numbers. Unlike track events, you'll have several acres of warm up space, so pick anywhere you like to perform your warm up— though don't drift too far from everyone else, and particularly the officials who will notify the runners when the race is about to begin! 5-10 minutes before the scheduled start time, officials will gather the runners on the start line—usually with the faster runners at the front. They will also remind everyone of the course layout though there will be officials or markers along the route, so don't worry if you don't know every exact detail of the course.

Half Marathons/Marathons

Now we come to the largest-scale events by some way, with thousands of runners in attendance in 'smaller' events and over 35,000 in major races like the London Marathon. As you can imagine, a lot of preparation goes into these events, so the registration process starts months earlier than other types of competition—in some cases, you will need to be approved before you can enter a race. In the bigger races you will receive your competitor number and an electronic chip for individual timing in the post between one and four weeks before the event. The reason for the chip is that it can take over ten minutes to cross the start line in large marathons, so it would be unfair to take everyone's time from when the gun goes off. You will also receive instructions on what to do during the event, so read these carefully.

On the day of the race, make sure you leave plenty of time not just for travelling, but also for parking, queuing for the toilets and getting to the start line. Runners may be called to assemble on the start line up to 20 minutes before the start of the race, so bear this in mind as well. Finally, some of the bigger events require you to choose from several starting lines depending on the time that you are hoping to run—for example, in some half marathons they will have a start line for those likely to run 1 hour 30 minutes, and one for those hoping to achieve two hours. Though it will be tempting to start from a 'fast' section to try and keep up with the better runners at the meet, it is recommended that you stick with a pessimistic estimate to avoid upsetting faster runners by blocking them, or by destroying any hopes of you getting a good time by setting off far too quickly.

Open Track Meets

If you've decided to enter an open meet that's taking place at a 400m track, then race day is relatively simple. Hopefully you will have checked whether or not the event required prior registration—if it did, then bring your confirmation letter or simply state your name to the registrar of the event. If no registration before the event was needed, then just bring your entry fee and sign up on the day—you will be given a number to pin onto your running vest/shirt. With the informal nature of open meets, you are usually permitted to warm up on the track—as long as you don't interfere with races already running—and you can simply sign in at the start line around 5-10 minutes before your race is due off.

Club Track Meets

For this, we assume you know who your Team Manager is—if not, then find out as soon as possible! After you arrive at the venue, seek out your TM—you may not even need to do this part if you travelled with the rest of the team—and they will supply you with the numbers or letters that your team has been assigned. You won't need to register at a desk as your Manager will hand in a declaration sheet with the names of all your team's competitors. As far as warming up and signing in for the event goes, this is the same as the process during Open Meets—warming up can usually be done anywhere that won't interrupt an event already in progress, and you only need to go to the start line for your event to sign in and be ready for your race.

Track Championships

This incorporates County, University, National and even International Championships that take place at athletics tracks/stadia, as the rules are broadly the same—though the higher up the ladder you go, the stricter the rules. These competitions strictly enforce punctual registration, so aiming to get to the venue 15-30 minutes before the 'deadline' for your event would be recommended. Registration is similar to all track events, but you will almost always need to show the desk your confirmation of entry before they will give you your numbers. Warming up on the track is usually forbidden in this type of competition, though an area will be designated for athletes to prepare themselves for races—this could take the form of an indoor track, a sports hall, astroturf, etc. There are strict rules on signing in for your race, too—there will be a Call-Up Area, to which you will need to go to confirm your participation in your race, and from which you will be led to the start line for your event.

ii What Should I Take With me to Events?

Here we will list all of the things you *may* need to take with you on race day, in a rough descending order of commonness—i. e. the items at the top will be needed more or less anywhere, whereas the ones towards the bottom will only be required for certain types of events:

- Running vest or top—this is very important as most places won't allow you to race without one!

- Running shoes or spikes

- Training tops and bottoms to keep warm before you are called up to race

- Competitor number if you've been sent one (and safety pins)

- Confirmation of accepted entry—an email, an online payment receipt, a form, etc.

- Sports drinks and water

- Food—both for an energy boost before the race, and to recharge afterwards (see Part iii).

- Money for entry fees, parking, merchandise or refreshments

iii What Should I Eat Before and During my Event?

Before your event

First of all, make sure you eat on race day! Although your appetite may not be massive due to nerves before a race, eating before a competition is vital to ensure that you have enough energy to last the distance—even if that is only 100m.

As far as nutrition intake goes, races should be dealt with in a similar way to that of training sessions—though you may want to ensure that you eat a little earlier before a race than you would for training. This is because you will be working as hard as you possibly can during a race (something that isn't necessarily true during preparation), and eating too late will result in feeling bloated and heavy.

Generally, the latest that you will want to eat before a race is two hours, with sports drinks, water and very light, sugary snacks raising your glycogen levels in the meantime. Similarly to training, there are also different requirements depending on the time of day that you will be racing. If you have a morning race, then your intake won't be much different to any other day, as a medium-size breakfast will still be required—this may have to be eaten earlier than you're used to, to keep in with the guideline of eating a main meal no later than two hours before your race. Afternoon races will require either a large breakfast or a medium-sized one with a small lunch, with snacks helping you 'top up' your energy levels otherwise. Finally, for evening races we suggest that your largest meal of the day be in the mid-afternoon, or during lunch time, with something filling (such as a sandwich) around two hours before your scheduled race.

The day before the race is also an important time for preparation—we would advise having a good meal, high in carbohydrates, 24 hours before your competition. Also keep yourself hydrated in this period.

During your event

For those doing half-marathons and marathons, it is vital that you take on fluid during your race. There usually are several feeding stations dotted around the course where runners can pick up a drink or sports bar to consume while they run, so make sure that you take advantage of these and keep yourself from becoming dehydrated or exhausted.

We would say that it is a good idea to take on small amounts of fluid every 20 minutes or so during a race. Ideally, you will also have some carbohydrates for some extra topping up of energy—this could take the form of sports bars, isotonic drinks or even jelly beans.

iv What Should I do to Warm Up?

Our recommendation to arrive at your competition venue at least an hour before your race isn't just so that you can become familiar with your surroundings or make sure that you register on time—you will need to warm up as well! Bearing in mind that some competitions require you to arrive at the call-up area—in which warming up may not be possible—up to 30 minutes before your race; you will need to put some time aside to ensure that your body is ready to cope with the rigours of your race.

You will hopefully have read Chapter 7, which explains the reasons for warming up, the basic science behind warming and stretching your body before undertaking strenuous exercise, and the exercises that you can do as part of the warm up. This section won't discuss individual stretches in detail, but will give general guidelines on what can be done before your race. Hopefully, you will have practised the specifics of your warm up routine during training sessions—this is important because (as long as you're warming up correctly) going into a race knowing exactly what to do beforehand can help ease the nerves, and if your training times are impressive, then why change a winning formula?

As we have said, the specific exercises, drills and even the order that you do them in are up to you, but we would recommend the following as essential components of a good warm up routine:

- A slow, easy jog to warm up—maybe a few laps of a track/field.

- Dynamic stretches—target the whole of the body, but the hamstrings, calves and hip flexors in particular are important.

- Drills to ensure that your muscles are put through the sort of effort that they will be during your race, but at short intervals as to not tire yourself out.

- Four to five 60—100m runs progressing to race pace.

Summary

✓ *Following these steps will help you turn your race day from a nerve-wracking experience into a fun, educational one. Experiment with different warm-up routines, different types of races, and different nutritional preparations to find what works best for you and run faster than ever before!*

✓ *Race days are both an exciting and a nerve-wracking experience. Ensure that you double check the rules of the competition and the expected registration time, whether on the event's website or in a registration pack sent to you by the organisers, so that you can eliminate any further stress about arriving on time.*

✓ *Your running kit and running shoes are obvious essential items to take with you to a competition. Other than that, the only other 'compulsory' item for some events is a proof of registration, but you will probably want to factor in the need for food and drink and keeping warm as well.*

✓ *Make sure to eat and drink on race day to give yourself fuel for the event. Eat the last main meal before your race (i. e. breakfast if the race is at 10am, lunch if it's after 1pm, etc.) two hours prior to your start time. After that, and during your race if you have an opportunity/time to, only take on fluids or energy bars for a sugar boost.*

✓ *Remember your warm up! Ensure you give yourself enough time to warm up the vital muscle groups to avoid injury and a needless setback.*

Chapter 15

Screening

Runners all have their own idiosyncrasies—ways in which their bodies function and vary from other people. Some of these quirks will be good (or at least don't hinder your running) and some will be bad and will need to be addressed in order to perform at your best. Some may even be severe enough to cause injury if left untreated. Finding out what shape your body is in is where a running screening can come in handy.

i What is a Running Screening?

A Screening is usually performed by a physiotherapist or someone who otherwise specialises in human biomechanics. It is a process of analysing where your body is strong and weak, or where it is flexible or inflexible. The aims are to reduce the risk of injury in the future, and to increase your performance wherever possible. There are a number of tests that can be performed in order to determine what strengths and weaknesses you have, and we have picked a few to give you an idea of what can happen:

Overhead Squat Test

Performing an overhead squat is just like doing the common 'squat' (i. e. legs shoulder-width apart, and lowering your body with a straight back until your upper/lower legs are at 90 degrees), but while holding a bar above your head with both hands. The bar can either have weights attached or not, but for a screening added weight is not necessary.

The test will look for a number of different things, such as whether your feet stay in the same position throughout, whether your knees buckle inwards/turn outwards/stay in a similar position throughout, whether your heels stay on the floor during the whole exercise, and whether your arms stay overhead or tend to drop. Many of these 'abilities' during the overhead squat exercise require strong core muscles and a good range of flexibility in your legs, so these areas would need to be looked at if you have any difficulty keeping your posture at any point during the squat.

Thomas Test

This test, named after a British surgeon, determines the length and flexibility of the muscles involved in hip flexion. To perform the exercise, you must lie on your back—usually on an examination table or bed—and bring one knee to your chest, while the other remains extended and hangs off the edge of the bed.

The Thomas Test has three main points that physicians/assessors will examine, with each one relating to the strength and flexibility of a certain hip muscle.

Glute Bridge Test

Your glutes—more-or-less another word for the muscles in your backside—will be among the strongest yet often most underused muscles in your body. This test aims to demonstrate the strength and endurance, or lack thereof, of your glutes through a simple exercise.

To perform the Glute Bridge test, you will need to lie on your back with your heels on the floor and your knees bent at 90 degrees. Then, lift your hips in the air by squeezing your glutes, until your body is straight from your knees to your shoulders. Finally, lift one leg in the air and hold it so that it's straight (and parallel with the upper part of your other leg). Hold this for five seconds, and then keeping alternating between your legs.

Having strong glutes will enable you to sprint faster, jump higher, and give your legs more endurance, so all types of runner would benefit from strength in this area. Furthermore, having inactive or 'weak' glutes forces your hamstrings and lower back to do more work while running, which is less productive and can increase the likelihood of injury down the line.

There is a whole range of tests for those carrying out running screenings to choose from, but the above should give you an idea of what sort of exercises you may be asked to perform and the sort of conclusions that physiotherapists/personal trainers can take from the results. Remember that running screenings are designed to help you and not 'catch' you out—there is no shame in being unable to perform an exercise very well. It simply means you have a weakness in the target area of that exercise, and doesn't mean that you don't have strengths in other parts of your body. In any case, having points to improve on is a good thing, as it means that we can always potentially run faster!

ii Is it Worth Getting Screened?

Ultimately, no athlete *needs* to get a running screening performed on them to carry out their training correctly and safely, so don't worry if you haven't ever considered it or if you feel intimidated by the prospect. That said, the findings from a screening can be useful to you in a way that few other things can, both in what it can reveal about your body and the depth of knowledge of your body's mechanisms.

We would say that getting a running screening would be particularly worthwhile for you if you are someone with a history of injury problems who is looking to start/come back to running. The screening may be able to get to the bottom of your problems, and you will receive advice on what to do to strengthen weaker areas. This information can then help you have an uninterrupted start to your running programme, without having to take a few weeks out to recover from the recurrence of injuries before you've even begun in earnest.

Summary

✓ *A running screening is designed to reveal strengths and weaknesses in each of your muscle groups, with this information being very useful for knowing exactly what areas of your body to work on to become more efficient and faster in your running.*

✓ *A screening isn't a necessity for runners, but it is recommended for those who have had a history of injuries and/or haven't had their body's mechanisms checked by a professional for a long time.*

Core and Circuit Training

Obviously, when someone mentions the word 'running', we immediately think 'legs'— that is the part of the body that is carrying us along after all! What we may not appreciate, however, is that upper body and core strength can be just as important in determining how fast you can run and how long for. Sufficient strength in those areas is also a vital component in being able to successfully carry out the most efficient running technique. Learning how to condition your upper body and core areas is therefore a worthwhile venture for all runners, and this chapter will talk you through why core and circuit training are important, while giving you a few examples of exercise—simple and advanced— that will help you along the way.

i Why is a Strong Upper Body Important?

A lot of problems that runners have with their technique are born from a lack of core or upper body strength—these problems could then potentially lead to an injury and a frustrating lay-off. A few examples of 'classic' technical problems as a result of upper body weakness are:

- *Twisting of the body while running*— a strong core will make it much easier to keep yourself stable and allow your feet to land in the correct position and at the correct angle.

- *Sitting while running*—the tendency to not raise your hips or keep yourself tall as you run could result from a lack of core strength. Strengthening that area should allow you to keep tall without much effort, and lengthen each stride that you take.

- *Tightness in shoulders*—this problem, whether due to poor technique or a lack of strength in your shoulders, can lead to quicker fatigue and problems in races.

It should be noted that we don't need a massively strong core, with no fat whatsoever and a six pack, in order to be efficient in our running technique—we just need to have enough strength and endurance to hold the spine in its correct position. The same can be said about your arms—bulging biceps are far from necessary, and simply having enough strength in your arms to match the effort that your legs are putting in is enough.

ii Core Exercises

So, we need a strong core to run at our full potential. How do we strengthen that part of the body though? There are a few workouts that are designed to improve stability in your central 'trunk' area, and these can be done as part of a training session or as a separate session in itself. Dedicating a session a week to improving your core stability is recommended, and this frequency should lead to your core strength developing so that you can run more efficiently.

The exercises that we will show you are commonly known as 'planks'—you may have heard of them or done them as part of an exercise class before, but we will guide you through the correct technique and advise you on what you should feel and where. Performing these exercises for a short while with good technique is much better than holding them for a long time with poor technique, so if you feel yourself slipping or drooping, then make sure you stop—even if this is only after 20-30 seconds.

Before you start

Prior to performing any of the exercises, you need to 'engage' your core, which will ensure that your technique and posture is correct during the core exercises. To do this, go onto all fours (i. e. have your hands and knees touching the ground) with your back straight. Now, lift your back upwards so that you create an arch, and then lower your back so that your spine sags slightly in the middle of your body. Half-way in between these two positions is your neutral, 'engaged' position—you should feel that there is tension in the area just below your navel. The same method can be used while lying prone on the ground or on your back, and those muscles in the 'engaged' position should be the ones contracted during each of the exercises that we suggest.

Front Plank

The first of the 'planks' or 'bridges' that we will suggest is the front plank. The preparation for this position involves lying on your front with your legs straight behind you and your elbows on the ground so that your lower arm is flat and facing straight in front of you (you can link your hands if you wish, though it isn't compulsory). You must then lift your torso and knees off the floor, with only your elbows and your feet supporting your weight (Figure 16.1 gives the correct posture). There must be as straight a line as possible all the way from your shoulders to your heels—if there isn't, then you are not performing the exercise correctly. Hold this position for as long as you can before you lose your posture—anywhere between 30 seconds and 1 minute would be a great workout!

Figure 16.1
Front Plank

Side Plank

This is one of the more complicated exercises as there are three types of rotation that need to be avoided.

To start this exercise, lie on your side with one foot in contact with the floor and the other resting on top. From here, lift yourself up to your upper arm so that your hips are now above the floor, and so that there is a straight line forming from your shoulders to your foot (Figure 16.2).

Figure 16.2
Side Plank

As well as this 'line', you will need to make sure that your hips are in line with your

shoulders—not bending too far forwards or backwards as demonstrated in Figure 16.3—and that your chest isn't rotating too much.

If you are performing a side plank perfectly, then an observer should see a straight line from the front, the side, and from above.

Back Bridge

In a refreshing change to the above two exercises, the back bridge is simple and generally easy to carry out. Lie on your back with your hands by your side, and lift yourself up so that your body rests on your heels and forearms, with your hips and your shoulders off the ground. The key position is to keep a straight line between your knees and your shoulders. You can try to make the exercise slightly harder by raising one leg—making sure that it is maintaining the straight line between your shoulders and knees (Figure 16.4) rather than being too high (Figure 16.5).

'Runners Legs'

This exercise requires the same starting position as the back bridge. From here, raise both your legs off the ground so that they are tucked in towards your midriff, and then straighten one leg fully with your foot around six inches from the floor—for explanation purposes, we will say that this is the right leg. Then, swap so that your left leg is straight and your right leg is bent. Carry on alternating until you have performed 5-10 repetitions on each side. Try to take around three seconds to swap positions—this exercise is not supposed to imitate a fast cycling action, so make sure you take it slowly.

Back Raises

This is another exercise that is fairly easy to perform, but may not be suitable for those with back problems. Lie on the floor on your stomach, with your hands to the side of your head or under your chin, and your toes touching the floor. Then, lift your head and shoulders as far as you can off the ground, while keeping your toes in contact with the ground. Repeating this up to 20 times would be a good starting point.

'Superman' Exercise

So-called by us due to its vague resemblance to the posture of the well-known superhero, this exercise is harder than it looks. The 'horse stance' is needed for this—i. e. your body should have four points of contact with the ground—both of your hands and both of your knees. Then, extend out an arm and the opposite leg fully, and keep your balance. After 20-30 seconds on one side, then swap arms/legs and hold for the same amount of time.

'Eggs in Baskets' Exercise

Also called 'Russian Twists', this exercise requires you to sit on the floor with your feet off the ground, while leaning back slightly. Then, you must touch the ground to one side with both of your hands together, then touch the other side. Keep alternating this for 40-60 repetitions overall. Once you become familiar with the technique or find it too easy, then adding a medicine ball into the mix to make it more of a challenge.

Though there are countless other exercises that can be done to improve your core and abdominal strength, the ones identified here are all easy to carry out and form a good base to build on—working on these once a week would be recommended. You can then progress by increasing the amount of time you hold a position (planks), increasing the amount of repetitions (back raises and 'runners legs'), or adding weights or medicine balls to your body weight ('eggs in baskets' exercise).

iii Circuit Training

In addition to core work that predominantly works on your abdominal area, there are a range of exercises you can do to help you build up lactic acid tolerance in your upper body (as well as your lower body, which is always an area that runners need to work on) —ultimately making you stronger in your arms, shoulders, chest, etc. These are commonly known as 'circuit' exercises, and they are a good introduction to resistance training (i. e. pulling or pushing a force) as they use only the athlete's body weight—so you won't have to splash out on expensive metal bars and plates for now! Having said that, dumbbells can be a useful tool to make some exercises more challenging if you're finding doing 10+ reps far too easy, so these are an inexpensive and easily-stored option for more experienced athletes.

The following exercises are the ones most commonly used by Momentum Sports for circuit training, and performing a selection of these (five to six should be plenty to start with) will give you a good all-round base to strengthen the weaker areas of your body and develop your speed and endurance. We have included exercises that strengthen your legs as well, as you will want to cover a whole range of areas to maximise the usefulness of a circuits session. In some cases, we have given suggestions on adaptations that can be made if you find a certain exercise too difficult or too simple. Where there aren't any specific suggestions, then a simple way of making it more suitable for you is to decrease/increase the number of repetitions.

Before you start a circuits session, you will need to be clear about what your aim for the session is. You will either be aiming to build up lactic tolerance in one or a group of muscles, or improve your strength in that area. The amount of repetitions will differ depending on your goal—for improving strength, only 10-15 repetitions of each exercise is enough, whereas more will be needed to increase your lactic tolerance.

Press Ups

Works on: Upper Body

Most people know of this exercise! Start with both hands on the ground in front of you, and lift your body so that there is as straight a line as possible between your hips, ankles and back of shoulders (Figure 16.6). Then, lower your chest until your chin is around five inches off the ground (Figure16.7), and return to the starting position.

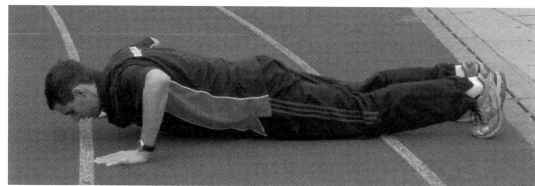

Figure 16.6 (top) Starting position for a Press Up

Figure 16.7 (bottom) Full depth of a Press Up

Too Easy?—try a 'Clap' Press Up. This involves lifting your whole body off the ground and clapping your hands together before returning to the normal press up position.

Too Hard? —go for a '¾' Press Up. This is similar to the normal press up, but your knees are on the ground. Make sure that there is still a straight line between your knees and shoulders, though!

Sit Ups

Works on: Torso

Another well-known exercise is the Sit Up, which builds muscular endurance in your abdominal area (Figure 16.8). To perform a Sit Up correctly, lie on your back, ensuring that your knees are slightly bent and that your hips are in contact with the ground. Then, with your arms either behind your head or crossed on your chest, lift your torso and return to the original position. Try to avoid 'pulling' on your head with your hands (Figure 16.9).

Figure 16.8 (left) A Sit Up

Figure 16.9 (right) Incorrect Sit Up

Too Easy? —With your hands behind your head, raise yourself to an upright position, but bring up one knee at the same time and touch it with your opposite elbow (i.e. left elbow touching right knee). Return to the original position and then swap sides.

Too Hard? —if you find 'normal' Sit Ups difficult, then use your arms to aid momentum as you sit upright, instead of having them static across your chest or behind your head.

Crunches

Works on: Abdominal muscles

To perform the abdominal crunch, lie on your back with your hands by your side. Then, curl up by raising your upper body while bringing your knees in toward you and return to the original position, trying to keep your feet at a similar height the whole time (i.e. a couple of inches above the ground).

Too Easy? —A slightly harder variation is to have your hands on the side of your head, and to raise your upper body a little higher than that of the normal crunch.

[Note: Don't use your hands to 'pull' your upper body forwards via the back of your legs.]

Hip Raises

Works on: Hamstrings, Glutes and Lower back

This exercise is both beneficial and simple, and will require a bench, chair or any other surface that is roughly 60cm off the ground. Lie on your back on the ground with your ankles on the elevated surface, and then raise your hips so that there is a straight line between your ankles and shoulders. Then, return to the original position and start again.

Triceps Dips

Works on: Arms

Triceps Dips are another exercise that requires an elevated surface of 60cm or so, and they help strengthen the triceps of the upper arm. With your hands on the elevated surface, elbows slightly flexed, an upright torso posture, and your legs straight, lower your body until it is at a 90 degree angle. Then push back to the starting position.

Burpees

Works on: Legs

Burpees are, in essence, two exercises combined—namely, a squat thrust and a jump. Start by crouching, with your hands on the ground. Then, keeping your back as flat as possible, extend your feet backwards and back towards your hands again in a jumping motion. The final part of the Burpee is to then immediately jump as high as you can in the air, and return to the original position upon landing.

Figure 16.10 The Three Phases of a Burpee

Half Squats

Works on: Upper Legs

For this exercise, your feet need to be at hip-width or slightly further apart, with your feet pointing forwards or slightly outward. Keeping your back flat and your head facing forward, bend your knees until the upper and lower parts of your legs are at 90 degrees. Ensure that your knees travel in line with your feet and that your heels remain flat to the floor throughout the exercise.

There are many exercises that you can do to improve your endurance in your upper and lower body, and these examples are just a small sample. They are, however, all well-known and relatively easy to carry out, so they are a very good choice for someone wanting to build up some strength in weaker areas early on in their running career.

Summary

✓   *A strong upper body is very important in a 'correct' running action. Many problems that typically occur for new runners stem from a weak core or weaknesses in the shoulders/neck. Dedicating some time to working on your upper body will bring benefits in the long run, as maintaining your posture will become easier and most of your efforts can therefore be concentrated on other areas of your technique.*

✓   *Core exercises and circuit training are effective methods of increasing your upper body strength. As with many exercises detailed in this book, start off with a light session and gradually increase the difficulty and workload—making sure that you can progress gradually over several weeks is much more preferable to giving yourself a heavy workout and suffering for up to a week afterwards.*

Chapter 17

Injuries and Illness

Unfortunately, there will more than likely come a time when you pick up an injury or are too ill to carry out training sessions. As a high-impact sport, overuse injuries and soreness from frequent 'pounding' on the ground are common, and cramps and blisters can occur now and again too. The Warm Up we do (see Chapter 10) and the running shoes we wear (see Chapter 1), and adopting the correct running technique (see Chapter 8) can help reduce the risk of injury significantly, but there are niggles that they simply can't prevent.

Should you find that you have injured yourself and the pain is not healing after a week, then seeking a physiotherapist would be the recommended action. As with other chapters in this book, the information here is not provided by a doctor or physiotherapist, but includes practical advice, and experience gained over several decades, that runners can use to cope with the disappointment of injury, as well as take measures to help the problem heal before having to spend money on specialist help (if this is possible).

i General Advice for Injuries

Some injuries will require specialist treatment or, in the very worst case scenario, surgery to repair the damage sufficiently, but a lot of injuries can be seen to without having to resort to paying for physiotherapist treatment or visiting the doctor. The most well-known course of action for 'minor' injuries is RICE—Rest, Ice, Compression and Elevation.

Rest

This part should be fairly obvious—don't do anything! As frustrating as it may be, resting entirely (even if exercise doesn't specifically work the injured area) will ensure that there is no aggravation to your injury—which could cause you to be out of action for a few more weeks – and will allow your body to use extra energy to repair the problem.

Ice

Anything frozen, but not so cold that it sticks to your skin, is adequate for this part—including frozen peas! Applying ice, wrapped in a towel, to the injured area reduces blood flow there, and avoids too much swelling through injured tissue. A period of 10-15 minutes of ice application at a time should be enough, depending on the size of the affected muscle. If the skin starts turning pink then you should remove the ice for a few minutes, as you'll actually be pulling in more blood to the area.

Compression

A bandage or anything that can wrap around the injured area will help reduce swelling further, and again help you get back on track as quickly as possible.

Elevation

As with the last two points, lifting the injured area—ideally above the height of your heart—will reduce swelling. If the injury is in your leg, then resting your leg on a chair arm or a pillow is a good idea—the latter can also be used to aid the recovery of your injury while you sleep.

As your recovery progresses, you should start moving to a period known as MICE, in which 'Rest' is replaced with 'Mobilisation'. Depending on the severity of the injury, this can be started only 24 hours after it was sustained, but will depend on whether you experience any sharp pains while moving. If you do, then immediately return back to RICE.

Mobilisation

This can take a number of forms, all of which should be undertaken extremely gently to avoid doing any significant further damage:

Walking—try to walk around normally if you can do so, as a limp can lead to injuries in other areas that are compensating for the reduced use of the injured area.

Stretching—try some light static stretching of the injured area. Again, stop immediately and ice the injury if you experience pain.

Treatment—after the initial period of RICE, you would ideally see a physiotherapist or sports masseur who would assess the injury and give you guidance on your rehabilitation; any appointment should only be after this initial period of care, as they are unlikely to be able to assess the injury before it has settled. The removal of scar tissue that forms after an injury occurs is one of the key things that a masseur will help you with to prevent future occurrences. Physiotherapists may also be able to help you with strength or mobility imbalances, which will reduce the injury risk further.

Strengthening—Once rehabilitation is under way, you should look at strengthening the area that was injured through stretching and circuit-type exercises, as the injury will have caused weakness or been a result of an inherent weakness in the first place. Physiotherapists and masseurs will also be able to advise you on this.

ii Common Injuries for Runners

Overall, there are a whole host of problems that could potentially occur, and listing each and every possibility would be impossible. Instead, the problems below are among the most common that runners experience, and we have included specific advice to treat and reduce the risk of each.

Shin Splints

What is it?

This is a common problem for those who regularly run on a hard surface, and refers to micro tears in the muscles that closely surround the shin bones, which over time can build up and cause stresses along the shin requiring treatment. Unfortunately, prolonged pain in the shins is something that we recommend you seek specialist help for in all circumstances—even if it turns out to be a minor, self-treatable problem—as serious damage can be done to both muscles and bones of the shin area, which can lead to stress fractures and a layoff of several months or even years, if shin splits are left untreated.

Causes

- Weakness in the muscles of the lower leg
- Changing the frequency or effort level of training too quickly
- A change of footwear
- Running on unfamiliar or hard surfaces without sufficient leg strength

Treatment

- Rest
- Ice
- Sports Massage—though it costs money, getting a highly experienced and qualified masseur to help will significantly speed up recovery—and you can also

receive personal biomechanical advice, which will identify and treat the exact cause of pain to ensure that problems do not reoccur.

- Self-Massage—massaging your leg yourself can also be very useful. This can be done by sitting with your right ankle resting on your left knee (or vice versa), and applying deep strokes up the edge of your shin bone from the toe to the knee. This will break down the scar tissue and release the muscles so that they work more efficiently. The use of a foam roller is recommended.

Preventative exercises

As mentioned above, the main cause of shin splints is overuse and weakness in the muscles of the lower leg which, when they tear, is due to a lack of flexibility and strength in those areas. We therefore want to make those muscles stronger and more flexible, and the following exercises are very useful in achieving this:

Lean with your back against a wall, with your feet about a foot away from it. Slowly raise your toes towards your shins so that you are on your heels, then lower them again. Repeat this 10-15 times, and then swap to the other leg

Step forward as normal, but only allow your heel to touch the floor. Step back and repeat 10 times

General jumping exercises can be useful—though you should aim to jump using your ankle movement, with your knee movement simply for cushioning each landing. Alter the height and speed of each jump for variation.

Calf stretches are good for improving flexibility. With one foot in front of the other, both toes pointing forwards and both heels on the ground (you can experiment with the distance between your feet – as long as you're following those three rules then it doesn't matter how far apart your legs are), lean forwards onto your front leg, and then swap after 10 seconds or so. Do this exercise first with a straight back leg, and then with your back leg bent at the knee.

Another exercise for flexibility is a shin stretch. It is a notoriously difficult area to stretch, but try kneeling down with your feet pointing straight behind you. If this doesn't feel like it's doing anything, then raise your feet off the ground—still aiming to point your feet straight, and not to either side.

Achilles Injuries

What are they?

The Achilles tendon connects our calf to our heel. Pain here is often down to training too much, and it is important not to ignore it as over time the tendon may become weaker and therefore become more likely to rupture—and this could result in a long lay-off. This rupture is not common but Achilles pain is and prevention is better than cure.

Causes

- Overtraining—training too much, too often.
- Can also be linked to a change in training (e. g. doing more speed work, changing surfaces, etc.)

Treatment

- RICE
- The next course of action should be to consult a sports masseur and determine whether or not rupture has occurred, or is at risk of occurring. This should take precedence over stretching the injured area, as you won't want to cause any more scar tissue to develop by overstretching damaged muscles.
- If you get the all-clear to begin MICE, then you should concentrate on stretching the calf and hamstring.
- In serious injuries wearing a stiff boot will help to reduce the movement of the ankle, thus facilitating the resting of the Achilles tendon.
- Self-massage of the Achilles tendon is notoriously difficult, so professional masseurs would be a necessity if you feel the area needs direct treatment. A masseur would be able to release the calf muscles and hamstrings, which often place significant strain on the Achilles.

Preventative Exercises

Strengthening the Achilles is important if you have a history of problems in that area. To do this, we need to maximise the amount of movement (primarily 'eccentric' movement) of the ankle muscles—this means exercises that lengthen a muscle under tension. Some examples of such exercises are as follows:

- Pick up a small object (such as a pen or coin) with your toes.
- Place a tennis/golf ball under the sole of your foot and massage.
- Eccentric knee squats—this involves squatting facing a wall. First of all, point your knees straight ahead of you and squat, and then squat with your knees pointing to the right, and finally to the left. You can try these on one leg too.
- Eccentric heel drops—to do these, stand on the edge of a step/elevated surface and slowly drop one heel.
- Balance on a wobble board, and try this with your eyes closed.

Things to watch out for

If you have a dent in your Achilles then you probably have a tear—in this case, see your physio or masseur for advice and treatment.

If you Achilles is hot or red and you have a temperature, then you may have an infection and should see your doctor as a precaution

If you experience tingling or numbness in your Achilles then it is likely that you have a neural problem and should see your masseur or physiotherapist.

Blisters

What are they?

Not an injury per se, but uncomfortable enough to affect your running and serious enough that you will want to avoid them as much as possible! Blisters are formed when excessive friction occurs between your foot and your footwear in one area. The heat generated from the friction separates the top layers of skin in that area, and the body then rapidly produces fluid to fill the 'wound'—the end result being a blister.

Cause

Ill-fitting footwear

Treatment

Most blisters heal naturally, so you probably won't need any medical attention unless the area becomes infected. Unfortunately, after a blister occurs the only thing you can do is manage it. Placing a plaster or any other dressing over the affected area is the best way to stop further friction from occurring and the risk of bursting the blister.

Preventative Measures

- Shoe fit—make sure that your trainers/spikes fit properly, as the slipping around of footwear creates the friction that causes blisters.
- Insoles—a special insole may help improve the fit and reduce the rubbing from a pair of shoes that are an unsuitable size. Many of them are breathable, padded and designed to be non-slipping.
- Socks—these are important in the prevention of blisters. Many socks are highly breathable, which keeps your foot cool and dry and thus prevents the build-up of moisture and heat that causes friction.
- Double-Layer Socks—an even more effective measure is to invest in socks with two layers (or wear two pairs of socks if you can!). The inner layer stays with the foot and the outer layer stays with the shoe, thus eliminating friction.

iii What is Sports Massage and is it Beneficial?

Sports Massage is becoming increasingly important for runners everywhere, whether an elite athlete or someone who simply runs for their local club. The main reasons for having a regular sports massage are injury prevention, or to speed up recovery if you have already picked up a niggle.

Injury Prevention

There are numerous ways in which masseurs can help you reduce the risk of injury. They can identify if you are training correctly or if the surface you're training on is suitable for your strength. For example, if you have been running on the camber of a road too much then this will show itself to a masseur through an imbalance and tilt of your pelvis and its associated muscles. They will then be able to release the areas of tension that would develop into an injury if untreated.

As well as current problems, masseurs will also be able to identify the areas that are naturally tight or weak and that could lead to an injury in the future. The massage will enable tight areas to be loosened and strengthened, which will allow the body to become more balanced and therefore less likely to become injured.

Finally, some injuries are brought about by overuse of a particular muscle, which often results in that muscle becoming sore and inflamed. Massage will reduce the likelihood of the muscle becoming overused in the first place, by reducing the initial inflammation that occurs after exercise and straightening out muscle fibres that may have become damaged. These measures therefore allow the otherwise overused muscle fibres to work productively and prevent them becoming strained or injured.

Recovery from Injury

If you find yourself carrying a niggle or missing training because of an injury, then massage can also be of assistance. If you have a soft tissue injury, such as a sprain, strain or repetitive stress injury, massage will increase the speed at which you recover, and will reduce the likelihood of any recurrence of problems in areas that have already been affected.

Most injuries result in scar tissue, which results from tears to usually straight and effective muscle fibre. When the muscle tissue rebuilds itself, it does so in a 'mess' of fibres. These fibres are strong but are not effective for movement, and it becomes likely that the fibres around the injured mess will become strained and damaged in the future. Massage will return the fibres to their original formation, which will mean that they function normally again and the probability of suffering another injury to that area is reduced.

What to Expect from a Sports Massage

Your first session with a masseur will include an initial medical consultation, in which you will be asked questions about your past medical history, the nature of your injury and questions relating to your sporting background and current training regime. You may also have to demonstrate actions that you can/cannot perform without discomfort. Don't worry—the consultation isn't there to trick or test you, but for the masseur to narrow down what areas and muscles to work on!

A good masseur will start off easily so that you can get used to the feeling of a massage, but may eventually need to work deeply into the muscle tissues. This can cause pain, but if you feel very uncomfortable at any point then the masseur would be happy to alter the treatment. Though a bit of discomfort is common in a good, deep, effective massage, there are alternative treatments that are available if you feel in too much pain.

Finally, a good masseur will be able to advise you on ways to self-massage certain areas of your body (e. g. calves). This can be useful for times when minor discomfort occurs during/after competitions, or simply to help with your muscles' recovery in between appointments with a professional.

How often to get a massage

In short, the more you train, the more often a massage is recommended. A runner who trains two or three times a week would benefit from a massage once a month, with those who train almost every day ideally requiring one more often than that. Those with an injury will be advised by their masseur on how often they should have appointments, but the number is naturally going to be higher than for athletes without any injury problems.

It is advisable that you don't have your first ever massage just before a competition. Everyone reacts to massage treatment in different ways, and it would be best to discover how you react to it during a training period instead!

Final considerations

Of course, massages cost money and this may be a cause of hesitation before you decide whether or not to book an appointment. Some masseurs offer a discount scheme, and you may be able to get a further discount if you are part of an athletics club and use an affiliated masseur, or a friend. We would argue however that massage is worth the price anyway. Without it, you may train in pain, will be more at risk of injuring yourself (which would set your training back several weeks at the very least), will take longer to recover from injuries, and will always be in danger of suffering a recurrence. For this reason, we would say that the advantages of having a massage far outweigh the disadvantages, so it is well worth getting one when you can.

Summary

✓ *Minor injuries, such as isolated pain or aching, can usually be overcome using the RICE and MICE methods.*

✓ *More serious injuries like muscle tears will most likely require a meeting with a physiotherapist to identify the problem, and to find out what exercises can be done to help with rehabilitation.*

✓ *Frequent sports massages will help you reduce the likelihood of injuries, or can aid your recovery if you have hurt yourself. Seeing a masseur may also lead to tips on self-massage, which can be useful to overcome minor problems in the future without spending money on a professional.*

Chapter 18

Joining a Club

i The Benefits of Joining a Club?

There are few better ways to motivate yourself to continue your running training and push yourself harder than joining an athletics/running club. No matter where you are in the UK, there will be a local running or athletics club that anyone can join—there are also several online directories that will be able to help you locate the one nearest to you.

Clubs can vary in what type of events they compete in, where they train, membership fees, etc. so it would be worth researching potential clubs before enquiring or obtaining a membership form. Nevertheless, the following paragraphs contain information on what you should generally expect to have to pay for and the benefits you may receive upon joining an athletics club—the advice we give on the former is actually the 'worst case scenario', and some clubs may have an even simpler application process! Conversely, the benefits that we mention may not necessarily be true of all clubs, but they have all been offered as membership 'perks' at some time over the past few years; you should be able to get clarification from a club committee member in any case.

Joining a club is usually as simple as enquiring via email or in person, and then filling out a registration form with the club's Membership Secretary. Clubs require an annual membership fee, while the first payment usually includes a club vest and registration with the national governing body, which will allow you to represent your club in local, regional and national events. This is optional if you don't wish to compete, or you want to only compete in open meets—the initial fee therefore may be more expensive than the annual membership.

Once you are a member of an athletics club, then you potentially will have several benefits open to you:

Running shops will often have discounts for members of local running clubs, so you can pick up useful running equipment and clothing for a cheaper price.

Physiotherapists and masseurs may also have discounted rates for members of sports clubs, which will make any injuries you pick up less expensive to treat.

If your club trains at a track or another place that requires an entry fee, then you may get a discount or special offer if you are a member of the club that is based there.

Finally, many clubs will assign you to a group to train with after having joined, so you will gain training partners to socialise with and pit yourself against!

Joining a club is worthwhile if you're looking to get more serious with your running. Even if you don't necessarily want to compete, being part of a running group with a sense of togetherness can help inspire you to run harder in training and to make yourself stronger and fitter—nobody likes being left behind after all! Finally, if you don't feel confident about setting your own training schedule, then the sessions that your new coach sets for the group can either give you some ideas, or do the whole work for you. Bear in mind, though, that sessions set for a whole group may not take individual needs into account, so you may find that you will need to discuss any points that you're worried about with your coach to make sure that your training is suitable to help you improve.

chapter 19

Training for the Older Athlete

The beauty of running is that it can be taken up at any age. There are plenty of Masters competitions available for those over the age of 35, with age groups in 5-year increments without any real age limit, so you won't have to feel that you're intruding on a sport dominated by younger athletes. Even longer races such as marathons, in which every competitor runs against each other regardless of age or gender, may have prizes for the first 'veteran' crossing the line.

As sports science progresses and we understand more about how our bodies work, athletes that are considered 'veterans' are producing more and more impressive results, with 40 year olds breaking 21 seconds for the 200m and over 70s running sub three hours for the marathon, so you may find that you get one over your younger peers!

There are, however, some concerns that older athletes have that their younger counterparts may not, so there are different considerations and recommendations that senior members of the running community must take if they are to succeed.

i Considerations for Older Runners

The main difference between older and younger runners is that, generally, the older you are the longer it takes to recover from injuries. One of the main objectives for veterans who are taking up running is to not get injured—this may seem obvious, but an injury that a teenager could shake off in a week could take a month for older runners, so it is even more vital that older runners protect themselves while they are training.

Older runners can also find starting their training to be problematic if they haven't had an active or sporty lifestyle for a long time. Years of inactivity, or certainly years of activity non-specific to running, can lead to a lack of strength in key areas and poor balance or technique, which in turn can lead to an increased risk of injuries. This problem could also be found in those who have had bad injuries in the past, or recurring injuries in a specific area—extra care may need to be taken when you start up, to make sure that your body can cope with the demands that you are putting on it, and you will need to make sure that your technique is good enough to prevent you putting undue pressure on weak areas of the body.

ii What Can I do to Overcome These Problems?

The answer to this question is to train smarter! Whereas younger runners will be able to train hard and often, older athletes will find it beneficial to tone down the amount of effort needed to complete a session, but to train consistently and optimise the attributes you have—experience, listening to your body—to run at optimum performance as much as possible.

There are a number of steps worth taking to help maintain consistent training, some of which are obvious, with others less so. Still, doing some or all of the following will help you run better:

Don't make big jumps in training intensity—now, this is true for all athletes, but whereas a younger athlete can make weekly increases of 10% and manage, older runners should be even more cautious when increasing the workload and overall distance of their training.

Try to run on soft surfaces where possible, as this can reduce the risk of injury.

Work on strength and technique—again, this is something that everyone should do, but this is often ignored by a lot of people so it's worth mentioning again! In short, working on your strength and technique will (if you do it correctly) allow you to run for longer, and faster, without succumbing to injuries.

Maintain fluids and eat well—the older you are, the easier it is to retain fat, so sensible eating can be even more important.

Spend some extra time finding suitable running shoes—nowadays, you can get shoes tailor made for any foot shape, size or landing position, so making sure that your shoes compliment your running style will give you a very good start!

If you are very tired, then don't be afraid to take an extra day off to recover—remember, we want to train smarter, and knowing when your body has had enough and needs to recharge is a big part of that.

On a similar note, learn what adaptations to make to your training depending on what your body is telling you—Chapter 6's guide will help, but you may want to take 'bigger' measures to adapt your training, e. g. decreasing target times AND the distance you run, instead of just one.

You can do extra activities after training to help you recover quickly. Stretching, refuelling and even ice baths can all speed up the recovery process—this is another measure that all runners should take, but younger athletes can get away with it as their bodies are quicker at healing.

Most importantly—enjoy your running! Enjoying what you do and relishing the challenge is the best way of ensuring that running will become a lifelong pastime.

iii Age-Related Tables

It is no secret that, as we get older, our bodies can't quite keep up the same level of performance as they once could. You may find that keeping up with your younger peers gets ever harder as you reach your late thirties or beyond.

However, not achieving as fast a time as someone twenty years younger than you doesn't necessarily mean that your result was 'worse'. Just as there is little value in comparing the 100m time of the average 11 year old with the average 20 year-old, it is unfair to compare the results of a 40 year-old and a 60 year-old at face value. This is where age-related tables come into play.

Age-Related tables are a way of finding out how well you are performing for your age. Using a grading system provided by World Masters Athletics, your time for a particular distance event is represented as a percentage of what would be considered the 'best' possible time for your age over that distance. This can then be used to compare the times of two athletes of different ages, and discover who performed comparatively 'better' than the other.

The most commonly used Age-Related Table can be found at:

http://www.momentumsports.co.uk/TtWMATable.asp.

Final Thoughts

We hope that you will find this book useful during your first few weeks of running. There can be so many different areas to consider, and so many potential challenges that one can face, that the prospect of taking on a running training programme can be intimidating to newcomers.

Throughout this book, we have endeavoured to address any fears that you might have had about training, clothing, races, injuries, nutrition, and many other aspects of your running. With several decades of experience amongst our senior coaches, we are confident that the advice we have given throughout the book is practical for novices to running. We also believe that you will be well equipped to know how to deal with the sorts of difficult challenges that would otherwise be disheartening or demotivating for a beginner with no help to call upon.

Our guidance on running technique, warming up and circuit training will give you a good grounding in the technical aspects of running and, hopefully, will give you knowledge that very few beginners to running will have had in the past. All of the running drills and exercises that we have given will be beneficial to call upon during your training, so you will be able to develop your skills and improve your running technique very early on.

One point that we've stressed throughout the book is that running can be as inexpensive as you want it to be. There are many goods and services that runners can buy, and we have discussed the positives and negative of these with an open minded, independent viewpoint and an acknowledgement towards the potential cost. We realise that buying everything available to runners that could assist their training would quickly result in a very large expense, so we have tried to give alternative, cheaper examples where possible.

Running is a very versatile sport and one that is increasing in popularity, and we hope we will help you make the most of it and allow you to get full enjoyment from your training. We would be more than happy to answer any queries or read any comments you may have—please email coaches@momentumsports.co.uk.

All the best with your running.

15181598R00068

Printed in Poland
by Amazon Fulfillment
Poland Sp. z o.o., Wrocław